Averting a School Crisis

Averting a School Crisis

A Risk Management Guide on Preparedness for School Faculty and Parents

Cody M. Santiago

ROWMAN & LITTLEFIELD
Lanham • Boulder • New York • London

Published by Rowman & Littlefield
A wholly owned subsidiary of The Rowman & Littlefield Publishing Group, Inc.
4501 Forbes Boulevard, Suite 200, Lanham, Maryland 20706
www.rowman.com

Unit A, Whitacre Mews, 26–34 Stannary Street, London SE11 4AB

Copyright © 2018 by Cody M. Santiago

All rights reserved. No part of this book may be reproduced in any form or by any electronic or mechanical means, including information storage and retrieval systems, without written permission from the publisher, except by a reviewer who may quote passages in a review.

British Library Cataloguing in Publication Information Available

Library of Congress Cataloging-in-Publication Data Is Available

ISBN: 978-1-4758-4309-5 (cloth : alk. paper)
ISBN: 978-1-4758-4310-1 (pbk. : alk. paper)
ISBN: 978-1-4758-4311-8 (electronic)

To my mom and dad,
Dr. Robert Tabachini,
and those who helped me along the way.
Success takes a village.

Contents

Foreword		ix
Preface		xi
Introduction: It Can and Will Happen to You		1
1	Understanding How to Prepare	3
2	School Politics	13
3	The Incident Command System and Why You Should Care	19
4	The Meat and Potatoes of *the* Plan	29
5	Use What You Have	35
6	Emergency Scenarios to Consider	40
7	Special Events at Your School	52
8	School Transportation	57
9	Crisis Management	65
10	Testing Your Plans	70
11	The Prepared School You Hope to Become	76
References		81
Index		83
About the Author		87

Foreword

If we are genuinely serious about protecting our most precious resource, our children—our future—we must develop a culture of safety and security in our schools. Based on the terroristic violence that has plagued our schools in the past twenty years, it is no surprise that the most vulnerable, precious, and valuable beings of our society are at risk. Our children are the primary targets of violent criminals that have absolutely no consideration for human life of suffering.

Averting a School Crisis: A Risk Management Guide on Preparedness for School Faculty and Parents is an excellent resource of knowledge and guidance. This text was prepared for all members of a community, first responders, administrators, and teachers to serve as a resource to raise awareness and activities among our children and communities—a great starting block for a strong and effective school security plan.

Building resilience through being proactive, and planning and training for any emergency in our schools, is often not the top priority—and not because people don't care. It is normally skimmed over because of time, resources (expertise), money, local politics, and, primarily, complacency. The human brain is a natural filter—a "this could never happen here" mentality plagues most communities.

Averting a School Crisis outlines innovative ideas that can prepare any staff and community member at your school for potential threats. It provides step-by-step guidance on how to prevent, respond, mitigate, and recover from a crisis situation in our local schools. Creating a culture that is receptive to responding to crisis incidents, no matter the magnitude, will save lives.

Schools across the country must embrace these concepts and exercise them regularly. Build your community emergency response team and make this book a required reading as a starting point, to begin the process of program development.

Creating an emergency operation plan for an educational institution takes incredible coordination and collaboration between many agencies. Above all, it takes strong leadership and commitment across whole communities and professional organization, not just inside the school.

Mr. Cody Santiago's knowledge and logic are critical tools to use, not only in our schools but also in our daily lives. This young professional brings a new sense of energy and ideas, real commitment, and genuine concern to make our most precious and softest targets—our children—safe and secure.

Dr. Michael L. Hummel, PhD
Professor of Criminal Justice and Security Studies,
Municipal Police Officer, and Retired Military Officer

Preface

In today's world, our school district leaders are expected to be prepared to respond to emergencies to keep our children safe. Our educators are busy enough as it is. Having less time to get things done and more students to teach does not leave much time for anything else. On top of that, educators are expected to further their own education and earn continuing education credits. Now we are asking teachers and administrators to learn how to be first responders.

It seems like a hard thing to ask of our teachers. The people we charge with educating our future leaders are the same people we ask to learn to save lives and train for their worst day in a school. Essentially, we are asking teachers to be a part of a paradigm shift in our schools. It appears, almost daily, we can watch the news and somewhere in the United States that there was an emergency of some type in a school.

Natural disasters are enough to threaten the vulnerabilities in our schools. Add in the man-disaster factor and that is enough to make parents not want to send their kids to school. It cannot be stressed enough that waiting until an incident occurs is not acceptable to test your plans or find out how they work. This book will help lead the way in either beginning your school's emergency planning process or improving it.

I get asked all the time, "How in the world did you ever get started in school emergency preparedness?" My answer is never simple. Truthfully, school emergency preparedness is something I wandered into. I did not just wake up one day as an adolescent and say, "I want to be someone who is sought as an expert in school emergency preparedness."

From the time I was a child, I knew I wanted to be in emergency services. It was in my blood that I was bound to be some type of community servant. At first I wanted to be a police officer or a firefighter. Then September 11 happened. The Federal Emergency Management Agency started designing courses to help prepare all organizations for emergencies. For most, these new courses were dreadful. The facilitators asked us questions such as where we would get our fuel from if the world was ending and how would we feed our communities. Most said, "It'll never happen to us, not here." Then again, we never thought our own commercial airlines would be used against us.

Out of college, the job market was tough. I was competing against every other college student and, in the homeland security field, if you do not have a military background, you may as well not even apply. So, I took a job as an instructional aide at my high school alma mater. Knowing that my degree was in homeland security, and that I had a little bit of experience, the school district would always include me in its emergency drills, drug raids, and so forth.

As they brought me in and asked for my thoughts on some of their operations, I realized how huge of a vulnerability gap there is within schools and their emergency preparedness. It did not take me long to realize that I could use the skills I'd learned and apply many of them to schools.

Teachers and administrators take pride in their classrooms. They want to do the best they can to protect their students. That being said, they are so busy that it is hard for them to find the time to prioritize emergency preparedness. Today more than ever, we need not just our teachers, but our entire school staff to know their roles and what is expected of them during an emergency.

Eventually, that led me to earning a job with an insurance carrier that insures schools in property and liability. It gave me a chance to walk the halls of schools around the country to gauge how schools operate differently from one another. Some schools embrace an emergency preparedness culture, others are more hands-off. All schools will tell you that they have an emergency plan. Some will admit they are not ready for anything more than a fire drill. Others will try to convince you that they are ready for an active shooter scenario. Either way, both of those mind-sets can, and should, be changed.

The potential for emergencies in schools is real. Schools are often referred to as "soft targets." Many are and will continue to be with the thoughts of complacency that drown the mentalities of our school leaders. The thought process of all of our educators and administrators must change. If you do not try to prepare, if it is something that you do not prioritize, people will get hurt and the loss your school and community will face is immense.

Be proactive. There are a plethora of ways to improve your school's preparedness. It doesn't matter if you think your plans are fully developed or if you are just beginning. Mother Nature and "the bad guys" are always looking for your biggest vulnerability.

I challenge you. Start the conversation of preparedness in your school. Make your school a place where parents feel confident in your staff's ability to respond to any emergency in your school. Create an environment where staff take pride in wanting to be able to save lives during an emergency. It can be done, but nothing will change in schools regarding their preparedness for emergencies until we change *how* our schools prepare for emergencies.

Introduction
It Can and Will Happen to You

> The tragedy of life is often not in our failure, but rather in our complacency; not in our doing too much, but rather in our doing too little; not in our living above our ability, but rather in our living below our capacities.
>
> —Benjamin E. Mays,
> American Baptist minister

Imagine you are a teacher or an administrator at the local high school. It is a morning just like any other. The sun is shining, you drink your coffee, you watch the news, and then you are out the door and on your way to school. You say your "Good mornings" as the children all settle in for their school day. Attendance is taken as the morning announcements are being read. Soon enough, it is time to switch classes. Out of nowhere, chaos arises as gunshots are fired. Screaming echoes down the hall from both adults and children. Your heart sinks and your stomach is in your throat. You know that you have to act quickly.

Soon the gunshots end, and the following questions overwhelm the thought processes of your brain: Where is the shooter? How many shooters are there? Is it over? Is anyone hurt? Where can you go? What do you do with your students? What do you tell them? All of these questions will engulf your mind, and if there is no plan and your staff has not been trained, your day is about to get even worse.

In this scenario, the teachers, administrators, and other faculty members started their day like any other. However, the ending of their day would not be how they could have possibly imagined. Teachers tried to account for their students in their class. Administrators tried to glue together the facts of the unimaginable. First responders arriving on scene had no idea what they were getting themselves into. School district officials were assembling statements to the media and parents. Social media gave all sorts of statements, true and false. Now all the major news media are on your doorstep.

Talking about children getting hurt or children dying is one of the most uncomfortable conversations you can have as a faculty member at a school. Most people cannot fathom the idea of an individual wanting to hurt children, much less role-playing with their coworkers what they would do if an event like this were to occur. That barrier of discomfort must fall. If school districts, teachers, administrators, parents, and legislators truly want change in schools, the fear of discussing tragic events at schools or on school grounds must disappear.

It is also important to note that though active shooter situations are a popular topic of discussion in today's atmosphere of school preparedness, they should not be the only emergency for which your school prepares. Thinking outside the box is a critical first step in becoming aware of a school's vulnerabilities.

Schools across the nation remain unsafe every single day, and not solely from criminal or terroristic attacks but also from other threats that could interrupt the school day at any time. School district leaders must learn effective ways to prepare, mitigate, respond, and recover from any potential threat to their school. As district leaders take this more seriously, the conversation barrier and fear will disappear.

Emergency planning in school settings starts at the top. There are many obstacles to hurdle no matter what phase your school has developed into on the preparedness spectrum. Whether a school is starting from scratch in its planning or it has had sophisticated and well-thought-out plans for years, there is always something to be done to improve emergency preparedness.

Chapter One

Understanding How to Prepare

It wasn't raining when Noah built the arc.

—Howard Ruff,
economist

At the conclusion of chapter 1, readers will be able to:

- Explain how to begin the emergency planning process
- Explain what an emergency preparedness committee is and how it functions
- Explain what a risk assessment is

WHERE SHOULD YOU START?

School emergency planning begins with a conversation. This conversation can be generated by anyone who feels vulnerable or insecure within the confines of a school. A student may bring his or her fears to a teacher, guidance counselor, or administrator. A teacher may mention his or her everyday nightmares casually to his or her supervisor at a lunch table. A parent may raise his or her concerns at a public school board meeting. A school bus driver may post on social media how unprepared he or she thinks the district is for an emergency. Or worse yet, an incident can occur at your school, you have no plan, and your vulnerabilities are exposed because students got hurt or even killed.

The latter is not the time to begin to have these conversations. Timing for a meeting about school emergency preparedness could not be worse than during an actual emergency. Administrators and school district officials must keep an open mind when concerns are brought to them. Attention should be given to those who pour out their feelings because their concerns could potentially become a real situation, one that those same administrators may have to work through.

Once a conversation has been initiated, it is a good idea to establish a committee to begin this long, tedious, yet important process of emergency planning. Various levels of employees should be on this committee to give all perspectives of job scopes and daily tasks. The committee should consist of no more than five to ten employees. It is ideal to find a person from each role of the district.

A reasonable emergency preparedness committee should comprise the following:

- Top school district official(s)
- Teachers
- Custodians
- Bus drivers
- Guidance counselors
- Nurses
- Cafeteria supervisor
- Social worker(s)

Finding people who are willing to join this committee may be difficult at first. For most committees, it is time that is volunteered after school. If employees do not see the importance of preparing for a situation that may never happen, they will probably be reluctant to sit on this committee and offer their time.

For districts that have tough teachers' unions with clear Collective Bargaining Agreements, teachers may want to help but are unable to because their time is being donated at that point. It seems strange for people who are not teachers to grasp the concept of teachers refusing to join in on emergency planning because of contracts, but teachers' unions typically have more authority than individual teachers themselves.

A way around unions preventing faculty members donating their time to the emergency planning is to effectively use administrative days. If employees are paid during these days, it cannot be argued that they are still volunteering their time for the greater good. Emergency planning should become a scope of their jobs. Be mindful of their time, however. Teachers in today's world are typically asked to do more with less. Their time is valuable. A teacher may have upward of twenty-five to thirty-five students and minimal time to grade, lesson plan, and cover for other teachers during a typical school week. So, if a district were to use administrative days to start the emergency planning process, the majority of the day should not be used. Instead, multiple administrative days with less time may be more effective. This approach will also allow for employees to start thinking about potential scenarios.

You may find that even after you accommodate employees by paying them for their time and remain mindful of their workday activities, they are still reluctant to sit on the committee or give their input. This is why it is so important to have emergency planning in their job descriptions when they are hired. Emergency planning should be everyone's job.

If faculty members are still not giving you their best effort or are still not concerned, it may be time to do what is called "burn their house down." During my time at Glatfelter Public Practice, Bill Raab, the director of risk management, encouraged his staff to "burn our clients' houses down." Of course, this is meant metaphorically, not literally, but it is the point where the reluctant faculty members need to understand the importance of why they are being asked to contribute to the emergency planning discussion.

Burning someone's house down means giving them a scenario where they feel vulnerable at work. The idea is to make them feel uncomfortable without embarrassing them so that they too feel the need to join in on the emergency planning mission. A scenario may be given to a teacher such as the following.

Scenario 1.1

> Mr. Smith, suppose you are at school one day and you are teaching geometry in third period. You knew when you were coming into work that day that there were supposed to be terrible storms, a few that could be severe. You look outside and can tell that the storms are worse than you thought. All of a sudden, the large oak tree that is in the middle of the courtyard comes crashing down the 400 wing hallway where your classroom is located. You hear students screaming and crying. A classroom has been crushed. What do you do? Do you help the students who are hurt? Do you take your students outside? What about the students in the hallway? Where should those students go, and how do they get accounted for? How do we get them safely back to their parents or legal guardians?

If emergency planning has not been a priority and faculty members have not been tested, more likely than not Mr. Smith is going to be feeling pretty vulnerable. He will probably be ready to join in on the emergency planning at that time. If not, it may take a few scenarios to get him feeling that way, and that is OK. Walk the halls and come up with some scenarios that would put the school in potential chaos.

THE COMMITTEE IS ESTABLISHED, NOW WHAT?

Once your emergency planning committee members have been identified, it is important to go into the first session with an intent. The idea of this first meeting is to create goals and objectives toward an emergency plan where all staff members know their role, what resources the district has, and what the district is capable of.

Goals should be set to give a clear path to success of your end result of emergency planning. Objectives within those goals should be created to identify what needs to be done in order to achieve those goals.

Example:

Goal 1—Create an Emergency Preparedness Committee
- Objective 1—Create an emergency preparedness committee consisting of the positions of . . .
- Objective 2—The committee will hold monthly meetings run by the superintendent

Goal 2—Write an Emergency Operation Plan
- Objective 1—Identify physical and operational vulnerabilities
  - Conduct a full risk assessment and written report to identify key areas for which to plan
- Objective 2—Establish a chain of command

It does not matter how many goals the committee wants to create as long as there are objectives on how to get to those goals. However often the committee decides to meet, it is imperative that someone records minutes of the meeting to keep track of conversations, to-do lists, and items to be completed by the next meeting.

WHO SHOULD BE INVOLVED?

At the discretion of the preparedness committee and at some point early on in the process, the committee members should start considering which community members should be involved in planning. The district will probably not be left out to dry if someone dials 911 and says there is an emergency at the school. First responders will arrive, they will do what they are trained to do, they will manage the emergency and keep administrators informed.

The committee may find that they want to invite all emergency responders:

- Fire
- Emergency medical services
- Police
- Special task forces
- Local emergency managers
- Hospital staff
- County communications staff
- Local grocers, clothing banks, and so forth

Not all emergencies may start at the school. One emergency may be a huge storm that rolls through the community and the local municipality needs to use the school as a shelter. It is easier to plan for an event like that before it happens, which is why it is important to include as many of the key stakeholders as possible.

Aside from the first responders, the local emergency manager would likely want to know what the district facilities are capable of, who to plan for, and how to manage transportation efforts, if needed. Hospital staff should be included to identify how mass casualty situations will go, how students will be connected at the hospital with their parents, and to go over important items like Health Insurance Portability and Accountability Act.

Just remember that when it comes to emergency planning, no matter where your school is in the process, it takes a village. That "village" should not just consist of school-related officials, students, and parents but also anybody who will be there in your school's worst hour.

When you include a community in on your plans, you allow experts to give insight on how they can help support the school's capabilities and needs. They also may even be able to offer suggestions on how to create a safer school environment or help to put incident-specific plans together.

Do not confuse community stakeholder inclusion for distribution of your plans. Yes, community representatives from various organizations should be present in your planning, but at no point should your plans be posted in their entirety for the public to see. Some may see this as a lack of transparency, but for operational security, it is imperative that this process, and any documents created therein, is not shared with those who are not in the need-to-know.

Do not be afraid to ask for help. Ultimately, remember the goals that the committee has created. Take the initiative to improve your school's security by bringing in community subject matter experts like police officers or firefighters, and also any community organizations that support your needs and operations.

WHAT SHOULD YOU PLAN FOR?

For most schools, emergency planning begins with a popular emergency in current events. In today's atmosphere, an example of this would be active shooters. Slowly, the planning process has transitioned to other pieces like parent reunification and even transportation. Again, this would go back to the fact that conversations that generate change usually come from a parent, student, or faculty member because they are troubled at the thought of a particular emergency.

In turn, it would look poorly if the school district did nothing to address concerns of student safety, so emergency planning commences. Even if a school begins the process by planning for the popular emergencies, as seen on TV, it is typically enough to generate other conversations to start thinking about other emergencies as well.

At that time, the school district should consider conducting a risk and vulnerability assessment. Because schools come in all shapes and sizes, they all decide differently on how the risk assessments will be done. Some schools can afford to hire a consultant who has experience in determining where risk lies the most within a district or organization. Others take on the task themselves. No matter if a school hires a consultant or it does it on its own, the risk assessment portion of the planning process is an important component.

Risk can be described as a situation involving exposure to danger. Risk is in every single person's life every single day. Every decision that is made, every policy that does not exist, every conversation that is had are all risks. Anything that is seen on the news that becomes a headline started as a risk, no matter the result, something at some point could have been controlled.

Understanding why a district should prepare is equivalent to the district actually taking the steps to prepare in the first place. Similar to the goals compiled by the committee, a risk and vulnerability assessment will determine where the most effort should be placed when considering emergency plans. It is impossible for any organization to plan for every single risk exposure that exists. If the district can determine where its biggest risks are, the situations will likely be easier to respond to if they hadn't been narrowed down from the other unlikely scenarios.

For example, if your school is built in the middle of a desert, it would probably be a waste of time to plan for a flood, unless flooding has happened in the past. Risk and vulnerability assessments can be complex, or they can be simple. There is no "one size fits all" for school risk and vulnerability assessments. Schools may hire a consultant to do an expert, in-depth, risk assessment, or they may just ask the emergency planning committee to determine, with logic and reasoning, what the district's three biggest risks are. No matter the approach, the planning process must begin with determining what emergencies for which to plan.

As daunting as a risk and vulnerability assessment sounds, it is only as simple or as complex as you decide to make it. A simple risk assessment can be conducted by evaluating a few areas such as history of events or incidents, the probability an event or incident could occur, and if it did occur how badly would it interrupt or affect your organization.

Based on table 1.1, you could say that the emergency preparedness committee for a school district met and discussed emergencies or

Table 1.1.

Incident	Probability	Criticality	Total
Bomb threat	3	3	6
Fire	1	4	5
Medical emergency	4	2	6

interruptions that members think would have the highest probability of happening or criticality of interruption of daily operations. There are no formal guidelines on how to identify and use the numbers in table 1.1. For instructional purposes, table 1.1 uses numbers one through five in the probability and criticality columns, one being the least likely or least critical and five being the most.

There is no single numerical system to follow; your committee can come up with its own. Table 1.1 is very simple. The probability plus criticality equals the sum. This table may not be as cut and dry. The committee may have a risk type that does not have a high sum, but they would still like to discuss it. That is perfectly OK.

Just because a risk is considered a low risk, that does not mean it is not important to plan for. Just the same, just because a risk may not happen a lot, that does not mean it should not be planned for. In fact, it may be important to embrace that low-frequency risk because more than likely your school may not have any experience handling and responding to those types of incidents.

According to table 1.1, a bomb threat has a "medium" level of probability that it could happen. If it were to happen, the hypothetical committee believes that it could have a moderate impact on the school's operations, based on them giving it a three in the criticality column.

In the far-right column is the sum of both the probability and criticality. The sum is especially important because it gives a moderate indication for what the school district should start preparing. One last element to consider in conjunction with probability, criticality, and the sum of both of those is the history of emergencies and incidents. If this same school district from table 1.1 has a sum of six for medical emergencies, and in an entire school year, they've had, what they consider, many medical emergencies last school year, they should probably begin with planning for medical emergencies. The same approach would be ideal for a situation that is not very likely, yet if it were to happen, it would completely halt school operations for more than an entire school day.

Though the use of this table is the most basic method of risk assessments, it is useful and practical. It allows for organizations to identify situations that they feel are probable and critical. The list of possible incidents can be as long or as few as the committee decides. It is at the discretion of the committee, and they should be encouraged to think of situations outside the box. Case studies from past emergencies at similar schools around the world should be researched to provide decent perspective into the possibilities of emergencies at your school.

Other schools may be so inclined as to hire a contractor whose specialty is to conduct risk assessments and hazard vulnerability assessments. Of course, this will cost money and has the potential to put a sizeable dent in your school's budget. Conversely, your school cannot begin to properly prepare until you recognize what your hazards and threats are.

In-depth risk assessments can be helpful. For anyone who has ever read a hazard vulnerability or risk assessment report, it can seem like a history book for your organization. While that may be the case, somewhat, the ultimate purpose is to understand the history of events that have affected your organization as well as what *could* have happened.

Remember that the basis for conducting a risk assessment of any kind is to identify your planning needs and goals. There are no rules when it comes to risk and hazard identification, only guidelines to help the planners through the process. Once the emergency preparedness committee feels that a risk assessment is complete and sufficient, the planning shall begin.

The goal of your risk assessment is to find what exposures and potentials you will most likely face or incidents that would be most detrimental to your school. The threat and risk identification phase is one of the most important phases of the emergency planning process. Emergency planning is like a marathon, so in conducting your risk assessment, whether internally or externally, take your time. Once it is complete, present it to the necessary personnel and have another discussion. It is tremendously vital that everybody involved in the emergency planning process is informed on what the committee has done and plans to do. When the committee has presented the plan to district administrators, it is time to present it to the school board. Why? Because emergency planning and culture change start at the top.

CHAPTER 1 SUMMARY

No matter where the emergency preparedness conversation begins, it should be taken seriously by district administrators. Conversations can arise out of almost anywhere from recent news headlines to neighboring schools incurring emergency incidents to lunch table discussion, and worst of all, when your school is faced with an emergency.

It is every faculty member's responsibility to provide a safe and secure school learning environment. In order for faculty members to be prepared however, the district must take initiative. Every school should have an emergency planning committee, if yours does not, it is recommended that you, or a group of faculty members, approach the district leadership to get the process under way.

The next step is to have a risk assessment conducted internally or hire someone professionally outside of the district who will have no bias toward the operation or personnel. Any previous employees, friends, or family members should not be considered for the contract. The purpose of the threat and risk assessment is to identify planning needs and what situations the district should begin to prepare for first.

The final step in this ground floor stage is to present the conclusions of the risk assessment to the proper district personnel. There should be more than one presentation to allow for sufficient timing for presenting the material and answering in-depth questions from the audience. Large-group presentations typically will not be gainful because district officials do not always have time to sit in a room and discuss things, especially when a process is new. Take the time to meet with small groups of personnel who have similar jobs. Meet with the committee immediately after the risk assessment is complete, then with the district administrators, then meet with the school board. After all, you will need their support throughout the entire planning process, and it is better to gain their support right from the beginning.

CHAPTER 1 PERSONAL INVENTORY

1) Does your school currently have an emergency preparedness committee that meets at least quarterly?
    a. If so, who are the people on the committee and what are their roles on the committee? For what do they currently plan?
    b. If not, has your school every considered a planning committee specifically for emergency preparedness? Why or why not?
2) Have you or anyone in your district ever expressed safety and security concerns?
    a. What were the concerns?
    b. What has been done about the concerns?

3) Has your school ever conducted, or hired a consultant to conduct, a school threat and hazard risk assessment?
    a. If so, what were the conclusions?
    b. To whom were the conclusions presented?
    c. What actions were taken after the conclusions were presented?
    d. If no risk assessment was conducted, why not?

Chapter Two

School Politics

What you allow in your presence is your standard.

—Andy Stumpf,
U.S. Navy Seal

At the conclusion of chapter 2, readers will be able to:
- Identify problematic political disruptions in emergency planning
- Identify how school funding will affect prioritization
- Explain how to implement culture change within a school

Every school district or private school is different than school districts that neighbor them. Uniqueness among schools is common and is usually a good thing. We all understand some schools are considered the "good schools" and some schools are considered the "bad schools." But what makes schools this way? What criteria are there for deciding whether a school is a "good one" or a "bad one"? The answer is simple; there are no criteria. These questions in and of themselves require subjective answers.

One person may claim a district's taxes are too high, and his or her neighbor may rebut that the district's state test scores are through the roof so it is worth it. Someone may say a school has too much criminal activity, while another person who just moved from a high crime area would say the crime levels are far lower than his or her previous school. The point is that whether a school is a "good school" or a "bad school" is relative. Data can be driven in whatever direction the theorist wants it to go.

The better and more specific question is how prepared is your school for an emergency? Again, many people will probably disagree on why a district is or is not prepared for an incident. When starting an emergency planning committee, these are some questions that are essential to discuss.

School politics play a vital role in what gets done and what gets put on the back burner. Typically, school leadership has a lot to do with why a school does what it does. Usually, *it* starts at the top. *It* refers to how a school operates, how organized the school is, and what the faculty thinks of their leadership. Staff attitudes, workloads, and school pride typically start at the top. The *top* refers to superintendents, business administrators, principals, private school chief executive officers, and so forth. Essentially, the *top* is anyone who has any level of authority or decision-making abilities within the district.

Emergency planning is not always on a school district leader's radar. Typically, emergency planning is thought about but may not go any further than that. Other times it can be on a leader's mind, brought up in an executive session or staff meeting, but the idea of planning for emergencies is dismissed by his or her supervisor(s); and the idea goes no further.

Risk management is important within a school district. For leaders of our nation's schools, to embrace this is still a generally new concept. Managing all exposures and being receptive to vulnerabilities and fears should definitely be part of school district leaders' daily duties. There are a number of elements that affect what a school gets done or does not get done. Again, *it* starts at the top.

SCHOOL FUNDING

Across the nation, school districts and school boards are faced with managing yearly budgets to ensure the financial security of their respective districts. School funding is one of the difficult conversations that must take place within a school district. Our country's economy will always be in a state of ups and downs. There will always be a time when districts can afford more for less and then the next year be forced to furlough staff members and teachers.

School funding is something that drives our communities. Our local elected leaders and school board members must work tirelessly to make sure that budgets provide students with a quality education while compensating all of those who provide that education.

Often, it is reported that music and art programs are the first programs to go. While that may be the case, things like time and energy that are invested into emergency planning and what *may not ever happen* or *has never happened here* are put off until the next year. Then, not only are emergency preparedness efforts put on the back burner, but so are the thoughts and fears of those who had them previously. If a district decides to turn away from planning for emergencies, attention gets placed elsewhere. Those other projects may not be any less important, but when it comes to the health and safety of young lives, there is not much more that is paramount than planning for what *has never happened here*.

Many times, school district funding and budgeting is what drives curriculum, staffing, and extracurricular activities. To some, emergency planning may be considered extracurricular, until a moment arises when that same district wished it was more prepared.

Ultimately, school funding is one of many components that decides what gets done, and what must wait until tomorrow, or the next day, or the next to next day. Until finally, those days turn into months and those months into years. Use critical thinking to find ways to keep emergency preparedness at the helm of your school's operations.

PERSONAL AGENDAS

Though it may be difficult to understand why, emergency planning and preparedness in schools may not be thought of as important by district leadership. Excuses for the lack of planning can be attributed to the following:

> "I think the first responders probably have that under control. We have nobody formally trained in emergency preparedness."
>
> "We don't know where to begin the planning process, nor do we really have the time."
>
> "We can't afford to hire a contractor to do emergency planning for our district."
>
> "Our plans are sufficient and we do fire drills as required. We will be fine."

Ignorance is probably the best word to describe all of these statements, and these are just a few. It is not acceptable to think no emergency preparedness planning should occur when the district is responsible for hundreds to thousands of young lives each day. Nor is it acceptable to stick your head in the sand when an emergency does happen and then to claim "you didn't know."

Imagine having to look parents in their eyes and tell them that their child perished and you're sorry that you did not have any plans prepared for the incident. That would be a tough conversation to have with a parent who just lost a child. Emergencies cannot be prevented most of the time, but plans to respond to and recover from emergencies are absolutely necessary.

Personal agendas are another driving force behind what gets done in a district. If a superintendent is hired and he or she wants to start on a new mission, all it takes is a little persuasion of the board of directors and other people with authority and those things begin to get done. If a person leading a school district neglects to see the importance of emergency planning, you can almost bet that when something happens to that district, it will get ugly quickly.

As school board members, it is so important to remember when hiring school district leaders to hire someone who takes school safety and security seriously. Community members are also responsible for electing board members who will put school preparedness at the forefront of their agendas. Preparedness of any kind is always a community effort. Lack of planning is never just one person's fault; the fault lies within the community if plans are not in place.

Accountability of our leaders and elected officials needs be in effect. Board members and the public should be able to ask questions about preparedness and emergency services involvement in the district at any time, especially during the public comment portion of a public school board meeting.

VESTED INTEREST GROUPS

Vested interest groups are organized or well-known groups of people, who district leadership listens to carefully. Groups that are most commonly known as vested interest groups are groups like teachers' unions, parents, and parent–teacher organizations (PTOs/PTAs).

Decision-makers of the district typically have some type of obligation to keep groups like these happy, or mostly happy. If a teachers' union refuses to do any after-school work because it is not in their contract, you can almost bet that no teachers would help with your summer vacation full-scale emergency exercise. If a PTO says it has many concerns about school safety and security, and is able to provide examples of their fears, the district will likely take its points to heart. If a parent claims that something significant happened to his or her child at school, it may be a situational wake-up call for the school board and district leaders.

No matter what side of the fence these groups are on as far as emergency preparedness goes, it is almost certain that the district will hear these groups out and consider their thoughts very carefully.

CULTURE CHANGE

Culture change is extremely important when beginning the emergency process. Chances are, if your school is starting from scratch in the emergency planning process, professional consultants would grade your school's emergency procedures as below basic or "not conditionally recommended." There are many reasons why school emergency plans can be inadequate, unpractical, or just plain nonexistent.

Changing the culture of how your school, in its entirety, responds to any level of emergency can be difficult. Complacency and laziness are still widespread mind-sets in school district emergency response. If someone were to say "fire alarm," most would assume it is a drill and proceed out the exit that is posted in their rooms as the "normal exit." If someone were to say "someone left the backdoor open again," most would think a student was late and his or her friend let him or her in by propping open the back door. If your way of thinking does not change, you could unintentionally be putting your school at risk.

Each emergency should be treated differently. Firefighters are taught that no matter how many times they go to a facility for an automatic fire alarm, they should respond as if it were the "real deal," meaning something is seriously wrong and it is a real emergency. Soft targets, like schools, have no place for complacency. Any unusual circumstances or emergencies should be taken seriously as if it never happened before. No matter how many times the door is propped open, the policy should be followed to make sure the school is safe and secure. No matter how many times the fire alarm goes off for practice or accidentally, it should be treated as if it were a real emergency.

IT STARTS AT THE TOP

So how could a school that has never had emergency plans or a committee possibly ensure that district staff is doing all they can to provide a safe learning environment? No matter the size of the district, the demographics, or the budget, prioritized emergency planning is not always present. As discussed before, other elements of education take priority over the "what if's."

In order to create the culture change, it must be prioritized starting at the top of the leadership ladder must start at the top. This top-down approach is important, especially if the emergency planning committee is being initiated by those with little or no decision-making authority as far as district operations are concerned. If the planning committee is authorized and then tasked with creating emergency plans and exercises to test those plans, their ideas and implementations must be supported by district leadership. Many staff members may not see the importance of conducting emergency exercises or creating emergency plans, but if leadership can show that the committee's tasks are important and nonnegotiable, those staff members will be more apt to participate, even if unwillingly at first.

School district leaders and officials should always be involved in the emergency planning process. Even if only one top-level district administrator sits on the emergency planning committee, that is enough to keep other administrators informed. When an emergency arises, district officials will be sought out by the not only first responders for answers but the media as well. If district leaders can implement an emergency response culture that starts at the top, they will surely be able to trust other staff members to carry out their roles and responsibilities when an incident disrupts the district.

CHAPTER 2 SUMMARY

It may be difficult to get the emergency preparedness ball rolling at your school. It may take time for people to understand the importance of why change is occurring in the first place. However, if school leaders can show they fully back the emergency planning committee and participation with the plans and exercises that are required, the culture will change over time. The change will take patience and a lot of conversations with many people and groups, but you do not want to be the school that can only convince staff members the importance of an emergency plan after an emergency affects your school.

CHAPTER 2 PERSONAL INVENTORY

1) How would school politics play a role in your school's emergency planning process?
   a. Would politics positively or negatively affect the process?
   b. What would happen either way?
   c. What staff members can you foresee overlooking the emergency planning process?
2) Do you foresee school funding or budgeting being an issue for prioritization of emergency planning?
   a. Would staff members request to be paid for their additional time invested into emergency planning or exercises?
   b. How would you convince staff members to volunteer if they had to?
3) What special interest groups (PTO/PTA, teachers' unions, and parents) would be problematic in cooperation with preplanning for emergencies?

Chapter Three

The Incident Command System and Why You Should Care

> Surround yourself with the best people you can find, delegate authority, and don't interfere as long as the policy you've decided upon is being carried out.
>
> —Ronald Reagan,
> 40th president of the United States

At the conclusion of chapter 3, readers will be able to:

- Explain what the Incident Command System is
- Share the importance of ICS with their school(s)
- Identify what ICS positions could be filled by school staff
- Identify vulnerabilities in their staff's existing command and management structures
- Identify potential jurisdictional difficulties

Typically, when a local level emergency occurs, local emergency responders will need limited resources. If they would happen to exhaust their resources, they call their dispatcher and ask for whatever they need. In emergency services, this is a common conversation, but to educators, they may not have a clue to what first responders are referring.

Resources is a very broad term. To a firefighter, a resource could be rescue equipment, a specific piece of firefighting apparatus, or simply people. To a police officer, resources could mean physical security measures (barricades, bollards, barriers), or a specially trained task force.

To an educator during an emergency, *resources* would probably mean things like transportation, tables to set up check-in points, or more staff members to complete a task. Once all of these resources are allocated, however, how are they to be managed? How are items and people tracked? How do bills still get paid during downtime?

All of these questions are important and they can be difficult to answer, but they are manageable. That is why FEMA (the Federal Emergency Management Agency) developed the Incident Command System (ICS) after the September 11 attacks. ICS was created for large-scale incidents similar to the 9/11 attacks because many organizations had a vested interest in the response and recovery from those attacks. Just imagine at the World Trade Center facilities in Manhattan, how many stakeholders were involved in the response and recovery? The city of New York and its first responders were there: contractors, state and federal officials, business owners, first responders from all over the nation, and so on.

A system had to be created to be able to manage the planning, operations, logistics, and finances of large-scale incidents such as the ones that day. There are hundreds of books, classes, and college degrees devoted to planning for these types of incidents using ICS. ICS falls under a broader plan called the National Incident Management System (NIMS). Essentially, this system is how all entities *should* prepare to respond to emergencies. ICS is only a small part of NIMS, but it is essential for entities like schools again, to create that seamless emergency response.

A large-scale incident can be defined as an incident where multiple organizations combine their tactics, personnel, and resources to recover from an emergency. ICS helps to tear down silos between organizations and forces them to work together toward common objectives set by the leader of the incident called the incident commander (IC). These objectives are broad, but they are taken by lower-level chiefs, and those objectives turn into tasks for the boots on the ground to complete. ICS is important for a school's faculty to learn because not only will school faculty be able to recognize the terminology that emergency responders are using, but it will also create a seamless approach toward the response and recovery of an incident.

ICS for schools is as simple as this—know your role. Knowing your role during an emergency could save lives. If you do not know your role, it could cost people their lives. As a school principal, do you know what you should be doing when the fire department shows up? If you are not there, does your assistant principal or administrative assistant know what to do? This is where training and emergency planning become crucial. Being organized and having a plan can save lives, property, and money.

ILLUSTRATING ICS

If someone is completely unfamiliar with how ICS works, it is hard to conceptualize what positions exist and how the chain of command should work.

The Incident Command System and Why You Should Care 21

FEMA stipulates that a well-organized ICS chain should look similar to the one in figure 3.1. Without any ICS training, the general public could probably not explain what this chart is or what it means. The most important part is that they probably cannot tell you why it is so important.

Figure 3.1 allows an organization to plan ahead of time and identify what roles people will take if their daily jobs were to cease during an emergency. To be frank, when a school day is interrupted by an emergency, school faculty should no longer be wearing their "teacher hats." They should figuratively switch into their "ICS hats."

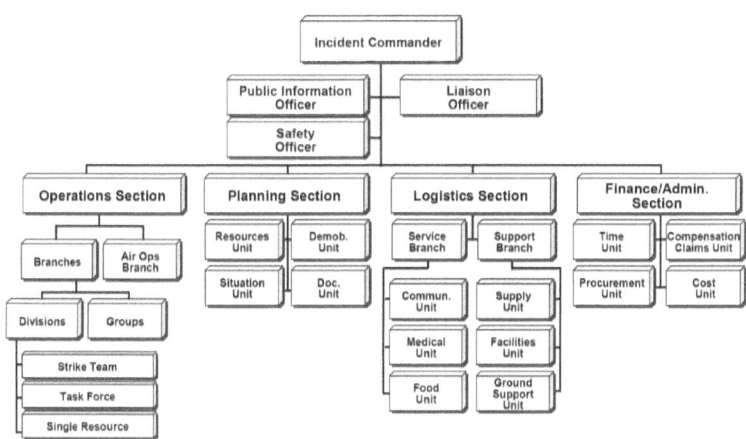

Figure 3.1. FEMA, ICS Structure, ICS Resources.

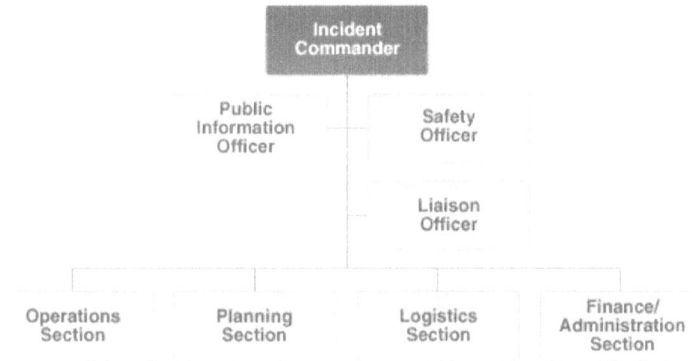

Figure 3.2. FEMA, IS 100.SCA, 2013.

Figure 3.2 accurately illustrates what an ICS chart would look like during a school emergency. This chart can be adapted for various situations, and the names of positions have to remain the same. Remember that it is important that your teams, names, and terms are tailored to your school and operation.

ICS TERMINOLOGY

Figure 3.3, derived from figure 3.2, is synonymous to what would be referred to as the IC. All too often, organizations get hung up on who the "person in charge" or the IC should be. Sometimes, districts discuss at length who the IC should be. Truth be told, any faculty member from your school should be prepared to be put in the IC role. It does not matter if they are a superintendent, a building principal, or a cafeteria worker; they should be prepared by leadership to fill this role during an emergency.

This position is often misunderstood when referring to what responsibilities it has. An IC should not be a person who is making rescues, serving food, or even keeping accountability. Of course, lack of manpower and need to fill that role temporarily is sometimes a must. However, for extended incidents, any responsibility other than managing incident objectives is not the IC's job and should be delegated to another person.

When an emergency occurs, there are several priorities that an IC has, and much the same in a school environment. In terms of a school emergency, an IC should be sure to establish, or have someone else to establish, an accountability presence to keep track of where people and resources are. Next, they should conduct a brief size-up of what is going on and what has just happened. Questions that should be asked for a size-up are as follows:

- What kind of incident are we dealing with?
- How long ago did it happen?
- Is anyone hurt, trapped, or killed?
- If so, what are we going to do about it?

[School Commander]

Figure 3.3. FEMA, IS 100.SCA, 2013.

- What exposures do we have?
  - Are there any ruptured gas lines?
  - Is there fire?
  - Has a water line burst?
  - What type of vehicle hit the bus?
- What do we need in order to recover?
- Should we evacuate, shelter-in-place, or lockdown?

All of these questions are good initial thoughts an IC must be prepared to answer. A size-up is not limited to these questions and will vary depending on the emergency.

The bottom line for being an IC is that his or her job is about delegation. Deciding what has happened, what needs to be done, and who is going to do it is key to this role. Giving up tasks and responsibilities for mission success is critical.

The positions from figure 3.4 directly report to the IC. When referring to these positions, proper nomenclature is the "Command Staff." They are appropriately named because they work closely with the IC on incident objectives.

The public information officer (PIO) is often thought of as the person who updates the media. While that is an accurate depiction of a PIO, in today's world, his or her job is much more than just a TV spokesperson. The PIO should be in charge of managing and monitoring social media pages, regularly updating the media at scheduled times, and working with ICs and officials to collect accurate and meaningful facts about the incident. Sometimes the PIO is the person who is simply gathering the facts so that they can be drafted into a press release or statement delivered by an elected official, a leader, or spokesperson.

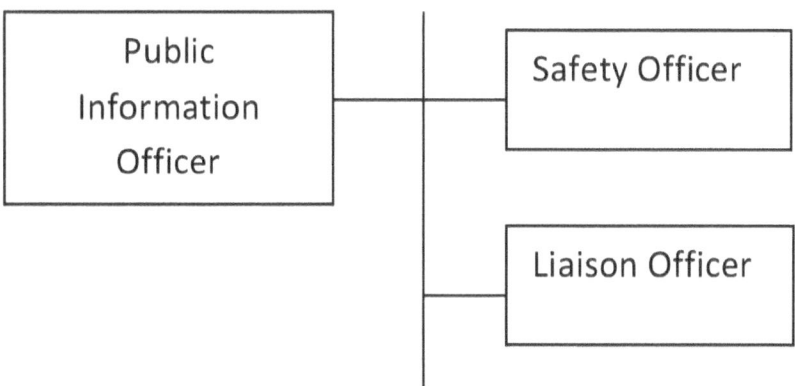

Figure 3.4. FEMA, IS 100.SCA, 2013.

The safety officer's responsibilities are exactly as the position title sounds. He or she is responsible for incident safety in all aspects. Depending on the incident, safety officers' priorities can range from managing exposures and alerting responders to monitoring traffic and access points for security. Ultimately, whatever the IC feels are necessary elements of safety for this incident are what the safety officer should focus on while watching for other potential risks.

The liaison officer is responsible for working with any stakeholders or anyone affected by the incident. For a school that may mean working with a local bus company to maintain the relationship for transportation needs, working with the Red Cross, or even with the police to advise the IC of other incidents that could interrupt the school's emergency operation. The liaison officer is simply in charge of talking to stakeholders that the incident will affect or with those who are willing to supply people and resources so the IC's time is not used poorly.

The rest of the positions shown in figure 3.5 are referred to as the "general staff." The positions of "operations," "planning," "logistics," and "finance/admin" are referred to as "section chiefs." Section chiefs are the people who are in charge of that branch. So, an "operations chief" is in charge of whatever the operations are. In figure 3.5, that chief would be in charge of managing the search and rescue operation, student care, medical, and security. For each box shown under "Operations," that box represents a person managing that task. That point is important because an operations chief should not necessarily be running the search and rescue operation. There should be a different person running the search and rescue operation, but the operations chief has the responsibility of meeting with all of the other operations branches (search and rescue, student care, medical, and security) so that he or she can report updates back to the IC. The same practice should be followed in all of the other sections as well.

Figure 3.5. FEMA, IS 100.SCA, 2013.

The operations section is the section that actually performs the objectives set by the IC. The other three sections are there to serve as the operations' support. Whatever the operations section needs to get its job done, the other sections are responsible for getting what they need, tracking the time and cost of the need, and figuring out how to deliver what they need.

There is not one ICS position that is more important than another. All positions in an ICS chart have roles and responsibilities. There have been cases where business and finance departments do not find the need to be a part of the emergency planning process. The fact of the matter is that, typically, they are the keepers of the "check book." If something needs to be purchased or a contractor needs to be paid, they will most definitely need to be involved. All memorandums of understanding are managed by the business and finance department as well. Any contract that stipulates that a contractor will provide goods or services during an emergency is managed by the business and finance department.

If any department resists, such as the business and finance department, remind them of what its roles would be in an emergency. Refer back to the section earlier in the book that talks about "burning someone's house down" and make that department feel vulnerable and needed in order to get its buy in.

Scenario 3.1

Utility crews have been working all morning in a trench less than 100 yards away from the entrance of your school. Your superintendent gets a phone call from a 911 dispatcher to inform them that the utility company has struck a gas line and it is blowing out natural gas.

The principal of the school pulls the fire alarm to initiate an evacuation. As students and faculty are evacuating, the fire department arrives on scene. The principal directs students past the main entrance and orders them to find a different exit point because of the close proximity of the school to the struck gas line.

Scenario 3.1 Questions

1. Who from your school will be the person to approach the fire chief?
2. What information should that person have ready for the emergency responders?
3. Because of the abnormal evacuation, how will people be accounted for?
4. Which faculty member(s) would be important to have near the school's IC?
5. Is it necessary to start assigning tasks to school personnel?
6. What are the objectives and tasks that need to be completed?

FIRST RESPONDERS ALREADY HAVE INCIDENT COMMAND, SO WE DON'T NEED ONE

Simply put, this statement is wrong. This is another common phrase that echoes throughout the educational atmosphere. The statement is similar to "The police are here and they have Incident Command, so we do not need an IC." The police are focused on safety for the public and the school. They are in charge of taking down the bad guys. They do not concern themselves with the school's continuity and restoration of operations.

ICS has a principle to eliminate this myth. It is called Unified Command (UC). UC is defined by FEMA as situations when more than one agency has incident jurisdiction or when incident cross jurisdictions (FEMA, 2008). In a school's case, the district is its own jurisdiction. Therefore, first responders may have an Incident Command Structure, but so should the school district.

The difference between the school's Incident Command Structure and the first responders' is that the objectives will differ for each jurisdiction. IC for the school will be managing school operations and the IC for first responders will be managing the incident itself. Though the objectives are not the same for each jurisdiction, the goal of safety and normalcy are.

If a first responder is running command and does not want to work with the school IC, what is stopping the school from maintaining its ICS structure and communicating the same way as if the ICs were working together as a UC? This scenario only stresses the importance of including the local emergency responders in your preincident planning.

Scenario 3.2

Using the same scenario as *Scenario #3.1*, the fire chief arrives on scene. You tell him or her the information you have available to you. He or she thanks you for your information and walks away.

1. Should you tell him or her that you are the school's IC?
2. Are you confident that your school wants you to be the IC?

Now your superintendent arrives on scene.

1. Will he or she be expecting to be the IC?
2. Is there a plan for who initial ICs are for these emergencies?
3. If the superintendent takes over as the IC, then what?

CROSS-TRAINING

Imagine if the person your school designated as the IC, like the building principal, is out on a personal day and a disruptive emergency occurs. The principal is out of town and cannot respond. Who is in charge? What if all of the leadership is out at a conference, who is in charge? What if only a few teachers, out of an entire staff of faculty, survived an active shooter situation, would one of those teachers be prepared to be the IC?

The cross-training of positions is vital for the success of the ICS structure. Cross-training is all about wearing different hats. It may not be in a teacher's contract to be an operations section chief, but when the occasion arises after the school has been attacked, will they want to take initiative? Their school is counting on them.

Put your people in the best position to be as successful as possible. Give them the opportunity to train and use the district's time wisely so that others may survive and time can be saved.

THE ICS OBJECTIVE FOR SCHOOLS

The main purpose of utilizing and practicing ICS regularly in your school is so it becomes part of the daily functions. It would be inconvenient in an emergency to tell a faculty member that he or she will be the liaison officer, and he or she does not remember what that position does. If ICS is regularly utilized in drills and workshops, faculty members will remain familiar with terminology and position responsibilities.

Knowing your role during an emergency can save time and lives. It also creates organization and leadership. If roles are known prior to an emergency, the chaos is already somewhat controlled. At that point, your people know what is expected of them and you can then focus on what needs to be done in order to return to normalcy.

CHAPTER 3 SUMMARY

If there were a better name for the ICS acronym, it would be Incident *Communication* System, instead of Incident Command System. Essentially, ICS is what improves communication with any organization that uses it. This chapter barely scrapes the surface with ICS. There are hundreds of courses on FEMA's Independent Study program that are free and many use the ICS principles.

FEMA has developed an ICS series that goes from 100–800. ICS 100, 200, 700, and 800 are online and are free. There are other online Independent Study programs that FEMA offers for entities like schools, churches, and volunteer organizations that are free as well. ICS 300 and 400 focus on expanding incidents and managing resources. School districts should require all faculty members, yes every single one of them, to take at least ICS 100, 200, and 700. These courses are online, they are free, and they will introduce your staff to ICS principles. Anybody who is in, what you would refer to at your school as a leadership position, should be sent to the free, week-long course of ICS 300 and 400.

ICS is a critical system that should be implemented in your school as soon as possible. The sooner it is implemented, the sooner your faculty members will become familiar and be ready for a large emergency that will disrupt a school day, week, or month. They will finally learn what it means to put their "ICS hat" on and know what is expected of them during an emergency.

CHAPTER 3 PERSONAL INVENTORY

1) Does your school already utilize the Incident Command Structure?
2) Who would fill the positions from your school that are listed in figure 3.2?
3) How often does your school work with local emergency responders to prepare for emergencies at your school?
4) Has your school ever had an emergency where an ICS approach would have been useful?

Chapter Four

The Meat and Potatoes of *the* Plan

Give me six hours to cut down a tree and I will spend the first four sharpening the axe.

—Abraham Lincoln,
16th president of the United States

At the conclusion of chapter 4, readers will be able to:

- Identify the parts of an emergency operations plan
- Logically reason what parts of the plan are relevant to their school
- Explain why each part of the plan is important
- Identify local and state laws regarding school emergency plans

At this point in the planning process, it seems as though you are ready to write or at least begin to assemble what your emergency plan should look like. Discussions have taken place, command structures have been agreed upon, and everything seems to be going in the right direction. It is time to begin writing your plan.

An emergency operations plan (EOP) is exactly what it sounds like. There are variations of emergency plans that serve different purposes. An emergency plan for your school should be referred to as an EOP because emergency planners, emergency responders, your state Emergency Management Agency (EMA), and FEMA remember that uniformity and common terminology is critical. Naming your plan "The Red Book Plan" or "Dooms Day Book" will do nothing but cause confusion, so just keep it simple. Emergency. Operations. Plan.

Your EOP should be tailored to your school's operations. It is not sufficient to find an existing plan, change the wording, and slap your school's name on the front. Most plans that are created as templates or are distributed by levels of government are too generic. They do not have the names of the positions that will be involved in the operations during an emergency and they do not use school specific terminology. Generic plans are not sufficient. It is OK to use them as a reference for formatting, but do not settle for complacency and use those templates as written. It is also OK to look online to find another EOP that has operations that are similar to your school, but be sure to only use the format and not the whole plan.

WHAT SHOULD BE IN YOUR PLAN?

There are a few important parts of EOPs that should be in every emergency plan. Other parts can be added if needed, but almost every plan has uniform parts. Those parts are as follows:

1) The Basic Plan
    a. Executive summary
    b. Purpose
    c. Scope of the document
    d. Implementation
    e. Record of changes
    f. Table of contents
    g. Concept of operations
2) Annexes
    a. Communications
    b. Evacuation plans
    c. Shelter-in-place
    d. Lockdown
    e. Accountability
    f. Family reunification
    g. Continuity of operations
3) Hazard Mitigation Analysis Results

(Guide for Developing High-Quality School Emergency Operations Plan, Washington, D.C., 2013)

THE BASIC PLAN

The Basic Plan is created to introduce your readers to the document. This part should explain why your plan is being created, how it is going to be implemented, and how you are going to maintain it. This portion of the plan allows the reader to understand the process that is being implemented. The Basic Plan also shows the *top-down buy-in* so that readers and exercisers of the plan understand its importance and priority in daily-school operations.

ANNEXES

Annexes give your emergency planning committee an opportunity to show how different your school is from the next. They illustrate how your school will communicate during an emergency and what methods of communication are back-ups in case the primary method fails. For instance, your school may use portable radios as an initial method of communication, but what happens when there is no power and you can no longer charge the batteries? Are staff cellphone numbers readily available? Where are they?

Annexes also allow for explanation of how your school will activate a lockdown or shelter-in-place and what the differences are between the two. This annex should describe what the criteria are for activating such a phase and the purpose of each operational change. Parents will want to know why their child's school is on lockdown or sheltering-in-place. The plan gives the school a reinforcement of decision-making in this case.

Other functional annexes to include are maps and floor plans. Maps and floor plans can become essential during emergency operations. This gives your school's IC a chance to show emergency responders what the layout of the school looks like, what exposures may affect a tactic, or access points.

There are many annexes that can be added to an EOP. Take pride in these annexes because they give you a chance to tailor your EOP to how your school actually operates.

EMERGENCY OPERATIONS PLANS AND THE LAW

According to the Justice Center of the Council of State Governments (CSG), there are thirty-three states that require their schools or school districts (depending on the state) to have emergency plans (Council of State Governments Justice Center, 2014). Typical topics in these school safety plans are fire and storm drills, active shooter drills, school building infrastructure requirements, and funding opportunities for school safety grants.

Some states, like Arizona, require that a school has an emergency planning committee. The committee is not only charged with the task of developing emergency plans, but it is also required to oversee the district's emergency operations to evaluate if procedures are being followed, directly reflecting what is in the emergency plans (CSG, 2). Other states, like Florida, have more

School Safety & Security Best Practices With Their Associated Indicators
2011-2012 School Safety and Security Self-Assessment Form

Safety Planning

4. **The district has implemented a school safety plan that includes district wide emergency and safety procedures and identifies those responsible for them.**

Indicators of Meeting the Best Practice

		Yes	No	In Progress	N/A
a.	The district has a school safety plan that includes goals and procedures to ensure that students are in orderly, disciplined classrooms conducive to learning.	Yes	No	In Progress	N/A
b.	The district has implemented a comprehensive school safety plan that establishes emergency and safety procedures for school and district employees and students to follow. At a minimum, the plan addresses • the evaluation of the principal's performance regarding school safety, monitoring and evaluating the implementation of the plan at the school level, and coordinating with local law enforcement and the Department of Juvenile Justice; [5] • the roles and responsibilities of the school principal and other administrators, teachers, and other school personnel for restoring, if necessary, and maintaining a safe, secure, and orderly school environment; • the roles and responsibilities of the transportation staff for restoring, if necessary, and maintaining a safe, secure, disciplined, and orderly bus environment; • the goals and objectives of the school resource officers, if any; • the mechanisms for identifying and serving the needs of students most at risk for engaging in disruptive and disorderly behavior; • arrangements to work with local emergency officials; [6] • safety issues and policies at school-sponsored events; [7] and • processes by which the district will instruct parents and the local community as to how to respond to an emergency situation. [8]	Yes	No	In Progress	N/A

Related Statutes and Rules
ss. 1006.10 and 1002.20(22), *F.S.*

Does the District Meet the Best Practice(explain if applicable)	Yes	No	In Progress	N/A

Strategies and Actions to Be Taken

Fiscal Impact and Timeline

---

[5] Principals may be evaluated on criteria such as the school climate report and school incident reports.
[6] Including, but not limited to, law enforcement, fire department, emergency management, hospital, mental health, health and social services agencies, court officials and the media.
[7] Such as when students are off campus at official school events.
[8] Parents and the community should be provided this information prior to an emergency through such mechanisms as newsletters and the district's website.

Figure 4.1. Florida Department of Education, 2012.

general state laws that allow for schools to simply *check the box*. Florida state statute *FLA. STAT. 1006.07* stipulates:

> The district school board shall provide for the proper accounting for all students, for the attendance and control of students at school, and for proper attention to health, safety, and other matters relating to the welfare of students including: [control of students, code of student conduct, student crime watch program, emergency drills and procedures; educational services in detention facilities; and Safety and Security Best Practices.

Does this statute not sound like how a school *should* operate on daily basis? The point is that this statute does not stipulate, in detail, what emergency plans should consist of. It is simply a general statement that gives protection to the health and welfare of students. However, the last portion of the statute, *Safety and Security Best Practices*, is key. The *Safety and Security Best Practices* is a document that has been designed by the Florida Department of Education (DOE). This document is essentially a fillable PDF for schools to evaluate if they have satisfactorily implemented documents and processes. The state is on a great track with evaluating whether schools have sufficient emergency plans. Figure 4.1 shows a sample page of the 32-page document.

For state government, this document is a great way to hold schools accountable for having any emergency plans at all. It is a foundational tool for schools to self-evaluate and for the enforcing agency, the Florida DOE, to evaluate whether schools are up to par. As great of an idea as this document is, there is one key component that cannot be measured: emergency preparedness culture.

The only culture this document talks about is culture regarding school climate with students. It evaluates programs for substance abuse and bullying. There is no evaluative metric that shows how a staff is effectively planning or regularly evaluating its school emergency preparedness. If there is no culture, no support, or prioritization of emergency preparedness from *the top*, emergency preparedness will simply remain as a box checking procedure.

Be sure to check the laws of your state and local governments on the applicability of school emergency preparedness regulations. Know what is required, but do not make your emergency plan all about what your state wants. Plan better than what any level of government wants you to because in the end, YOUR SCHOOL will be the one affected. Do not prepare for *them*, prepare for YOU.

CHAPTER 4 SUMMARY

Though an EOP can have many variations, the aforementioned elements are the foundations and necessities of each school EOP. There are many other parts that can be added based upon how your school functions, the types of positions, and even the type of school that you are. A military school will be much different than a catholic school. An inner-city school with a high rate of violence will have different components than a small rural school. When planning for your school's emergencies, statistics matter because those stats can more reliably predict what should be planned for, and thus, what should be in your plan.

Remember to use plain language at an intermediate reading level. These plans may not always be used during times of controlled chaos. They should be easily read so that they can be easily understood. Use common terminology, but also use terminology that is within the guidelines of things like the Incident Command Structure. If you must use acronyms, be sure to have an acronym glossary or identify what the acronym means directly after using the acronym.

Knowing what should go in your school's emergency plan, from a preparedness perspective, and what is required by law should be recognized. Include the elements necessary to follow your state's school emergency preparedness law(s), if there are any, but keep in mind that this is your school's plan. Take pride in knowing that. Parents, families, students, all rely on you during a time when people are hurt or in danger within your school. Don't use this plan to make your government happy. Use this plan to save lives, time, and money.

CHAPTER 4 PERSONAL INVENTORY

1) Does your school have an EOP?
    a. Do you know who wrote it?
    b. Do you know what is in it?
    c. Is the EOP ever practiced and then evaluated?
    d. Does it follow guidelines set forth by your state and by FEMA?
2) What laws does your state have on school emergency plans?
3) Does your state evaluate school emergency plans?
    a. If so, what is productive about the evaluation?
    b. What would you change about the evaluation?

Chapter Five

Use What You Have

Start where you are. Use what you have. Do what you can.

—Arthur Ashe,
American professional tennis player

At the conclusion of chapter 5, readers will be able to:

- Identify how to efficiently use school resources
- Identify who should be utilized during an emergency
- Explain the importance of utilizing school staff

Now that you understand how the ICS works, it is time to start placing your staff into those positions. However, do not just think about how to fill out the ICS structure. Think about applicability during an emergency or crisis at your school. Yes, the ICS structure looks nice and it should be utilized, but now it is time to think operationally school by school.

No matter if you are a school district managing a major emergency or a fire department, you have to understand the art of using the resources at your disposal. Your principal may want a professional crisis intervention team dispatched to your school during or after an emergency, but they may not arrive for hours or days. Your school nurse may tell you that he or she needs more stretchers to move injured staff and students, but the ambulance staff on scene has already used all of their stretchers.

The art of using what you have at a given point in an emergency is critical. How you get a job done may not be pretty, but at that point, does it matter as long as the situation is not worsening by doing what needs to be done?

Take for example the mass shooting at the Route 91 Festival in Las Vegas in 2017 where 58 people were killed and 489 additional people were wounded. In total, that is just shy of 550 people who needed immediate medical attention. There were not enough ambulances, medical staff, or stretchers to care for the victims. If you saw any news footage of the incident, you could see wounded victims being carried on things like fences and foldable tables by people who appeared to have no medical background or training. Though this particular incident did not occur at a school, it is a great example of how people used what they had to care for those who couldn't care for themselves.

Think of a scenario that would cause panic, disruption, and mass casualties at your school. It is a scary thought of course, but it is necessary to contemplate. Now think about who the best people would be to care for the wounded even if they have no medical training. Then think of someone who would not thrive in that environment. The good news during a bad situation is that there are roles for both of those personality types during an emergency.

BUILDING EMERGENCY RESPONSE TEAMS

Every school organization should have what is called a Building Emergency Response Team (BERT). A BERT is a group of school staff members with different roles that are utilized, as a team, for special assignments. The purpose of a BERT is to provide extra assistance to students and staff during an emergency and may also assist emergency responders.

The reason it is called a BERT is because each building or school in your district should have one of these teams. BERTs will vary in size and personnel depending on how many staff and students you have as well as the types of positions you have at your school.

An efficient BERT will have the following positions:

- Building principal(s)
- Teacher(s)
- Guidance counselor(s)
- Nurse(s)
- Administrative assistant(s)
- Custodian(s)
- Students who are volunteer firefighters, emergency medical technicians, lifeguards, and so forth.

A school that has 1,000 students in one building should have a larger BERT than that of a school with 200 students in it. No matter what, the BERT should be designed to fit your school's needs during an emergency. Note that the use of students is acceptable. These students should be identified before an incident occurs. Their involvement with the BERT should be announced to all other BERT members so they are not sent away during an emergency. Students who have training in emergency services areas could be very helpful during a major emergency. If your school is considering this, be sure to contact the parents and have them give their permission to allow their child to be involved with the BERT.

BERTs can be used in a number of ways. Be creative. Do not feel the need to limit your BERT's responses and activations to certain incidents. With that in mind, BERTs should not self-dispatch. In other words, they should be activated by someone with authority to do so, such as the building principal.

The use of BERTs should not be limited in their responses, but again, that is at the discretion of the district. Types of incidents to which BERT's could respond are as follows:

- Bus accidents
- Medical emergencies
- School attacks
- Structural collapse
- Parent reunification
- Evacuations

Though these are simply examples, get crafty in how to use your BERT. It will come in handy when needed.

Whatever situations your school decides to use your BERTs for is completely discretionary; however, the roles of each person should be clearly defined. Each person should know what his or her primary function is and what is expected of him or her. For example, a bus incident in the district may send school officials to the actual site to manage logistics of unharmed student transports and information gathering. The BERT team could be activated at the school to prepare for parent reunification. Exercises and training should take place frequently so that staff members are familiar with where they should be and what their jobs are.

HOW A BERT SHOULD WORK

If a school were to assemble a BERT, it is critically necessary that a chain of command be established. It is also necessary that only a few people in the building have the authority to activate the BERT. Strategically give authority to senior leadership at your building in different roles.

The reason for giving different staff members the ability to activate the BERT is in case certain staff members are not at work that day. For instance, if only your building principal has the authority to activate the BERT and he or she is at a conference all week, it could create confusion. Consider giving BERT activation authority to other staff members such as a guidance counselor, school nurse, and school resource officer.

FEMA's ICS stipulates that an efficient span of control is three to seven people, five being the optimum number. What that means is that for every three to seven people, one person should be in charge. Otherwise, operations, communication, and accountability are no longer efficient. An example is if your BERT has twenty people, they should be divided up into a few groups with a leader. Splitting of the BERT allows for teams to work in different areas of the school, if necessary, but also together if needed.

BERT TRAINING

Though we will get into school emergency exercises and training methods, training methods specific to the BERT are significantly important. BERTs should be trained as much as the rest of your staff, and even more because they are technically a special operations group. The group of people who are on your BERT probably already have special characteristics and traits that make them an important part of your school's operations.

It is a good idea to train this group in various areas of rescue, first aid, and teamwork, just to name a few. Get in contact with local emergency responders and have these people attend your in-house training sessions. This involvement also has the potential to improve your communications and relationships with those responders, which is vital to have before an emergency occurs. They may even be able to provide the training sessions for your staff.

USE ALL THE RESOURCES

Alluding to the incident in Las Vegas, as previously mentioned, you may not have what you need when an emergency occurs. In fact, it is almost given that you will not have who and what you need when an incident arises. Emergencies do not consider the weather, who is at work, or how busy emergency responders are. You and your school need to be prepared to think outside the box.

Buses can be a huge asset during emergencies. Depending on the incident, you may need a bus to transport uninjured students that were involved in a bus accident. You may need a bus to come to your school for an evacuation that may take hours. Use buses whenever you feel necessary, but just know that you have them in your arsenal of preparedness. Be prepared to use anyone and anything in any way you see as beneficial to a situation.

CHAPTER 5 SUMMARY

Use what you have. Do not wait until an emergency to decide how things get done. And do what it takes for your people to be trained. Doing these three simple things will save time, energy, lives, and money.

Establish a BERT and give incentives for people who join. Allow your first responder students to be involved and take initiative. Schools constantly beg their students to get involved in their communities, what better way to start than right in their school? Additionally, let your BERTs know what is expected of them, where to be when they are activated, and how they should communicate.

Ultimately, knowing what is available to you and thinking outside the box in the first moments of an emergency can save lives, time, and money. The more time you invest now in your people, your culture, and your planning, the less time you will spend dealing with the problems that occur due to your lack of planning.

CHAPTER 5 PERSONAL INVENTORY

1) Does your school already have a system similar to a BERT?
2) Who would be on your school's BERT?
3) What items do you think are important during an emergency at your school?
4) Has your school ever had to think outside the box during an emergency?
   a. What happened and how did it turn out?

Chapter Six

Emergency Scenarios to Consider

By failing to prepare, you are preparing to fail.

—Benjamin Franklin,
a Founding Father of the United States and an American innovator

At the conclusion of chapter 6, readers will be able to:

- Identify common scenarios that trouble most schools
- Reason on how to logically plan for their most probable or critical scenarios

If your school is ready to start seriously planning for emergencies, it is important to acknowledge that this phase of emergency planning is one of the most important phases. Surely, this is no surprise, but how your school decides to prepare for emergencies, and for what situations, that plan will then become a priority to the rest of the school organization. This is where your risk assessment comes into play. The scenarios that will be planned should be based upon your risk assessment and what scenarios your school is most concerned with.

Take your time during this phase. Allow for open and honest conversations. It is impossible to create a plan for every single scenario. Therefore, try to create plans that will work for more than one situation. Fire drills, lockdowns, lock-outs, or evacuation plans are a great example as they can be used for many different types of emergencies and so can lockdowns and shelter-in-place plans.

ACTIVE SHOOTER SCENARIO

This scenario is by far one of the most popular events for which to plan for any organization, not just schools. Active shooter situations are a hot topic for any organization responsible for people in the workplace or in educational environments on a daily basis.

The definition of an active shooter, which has been approved by several federal government departments, is "an individual actively engaged in killing or attempting to kill people in confined and populated areas"(Blair & Schweit, 2014). Active shooters attack schools for reasons that we, as a society, may never know.

Many organizations like to characterize the typical race, age, and gender of active shooters. Try not to get lost in the statistics when gathering facts. Data can be manipulated in any way that someone wants it to be perceived. In terms of preparedness, it will not matter what color the person is, how old he or she is, or if the person is male or female. What will matter is how you plan to respond while protecting students and staff.

In a study that was conducted by the Federal Bureau of Investigation (FBI), it was determined that out of 160 active shooter cases from the year 2000–2013, 24 percent (39/160) of all active shooter scenarios occurred in a school. Unfortunately, school shootings are no longer a surprise when the media blast these occurrences on TV and social media platforms. It is a sad reality that schools are an incredibly soft target. But with your help, you can help to harden the target.

Schools are an interesting place. Parents expect their children should *be* safe in school and should *feel* safe in school. There should be appropriate security measures, laws, accountability, district policies, and oversight in order to protect the children. However, it is not an ideal practice to start building or renovating schools to look like maximum security facilities. It is advisable to create a school environment that is the happy medium between a maximum-security facility and Disney World.

It is true that children are supposed to *be* and *feel* safe in school. They should also be excited to go to school and thrive in an encouraging educational environment. We can do better with how we prepare for emergencies, particularly active shooters, and how we design our schools. However, we should not begin to create a trend that turns schools into prison-like facilities. No matter how protected someone or a place may be, it will always be vulnerable to an attack.

Your school has the choice to decide if it wants to go on its own and create a tailored active shooter plan from scratch or choose to go the route of one of the hundreds of templated active shooter plans created by professionals.

Some common templated active shooter plans and training you may have heard of are *Run, Hide, Fight, ALICE,* or the *Standard Response Protocol.*

No matter which route your school decides to go, invest your time and energy into it so that the rest of the organization buys in. Remember that there are many programs out there. Some cost money, some are free. They all have pros and cons and many are probably not a good fit for your school; however, some will be a good fit. No matter if you choose to create your own plans from scratch or go with a templated program, do your research, make a decision, and then create buy in.

There is no *one-size-fits-all* plan out there. If you believe there is, more than likely, it is not going to work for your school. Templated plans are templated for a reason. They give you a great foundation and a program to follow, but the school district still has to do things on its end in order for these plans to even remotely work. Find or create a program that has a good lockdown and shelter-in-place process, a notification procedure that let's students and staff know when there is danger and when it is all clear, and finally the program must have a solid training piece so that everyone knows his or her role.

Remember that intelligent terrorists will find ways to compromise your system. They will try to do things like deceive your students and staff that the school is safe and they can come out of hiding or lockdown. If it is someone who works or attends your school, he or she will know major components of whatever plan you have. Plan for that to happen. Prepare to respond as if your first and second plans are out the window.

The final step in preparing for an active shooter is to practice. Whatever your plan is, share it with your students and staff. Once you have shared the plan, practice it. Once you have practiced the plan, revise it. Then practice it again, but this time throw some variables in so the situation is not "perfect." Then revise it again.

Active shooter and lone wolf attack situations are the most difficult scenario for which to plan. Often times, the actions of these attackers require minimal logistics plans because they are exposing an already vulnerable area or facility. Be prepared to think on the run, but do not wait to plan for these situations.

BOMB THREATS

Bomb threats made to a school can be a serious interruption to your operation. Threats can be made for a variety of reasons, but they are mainly intended for disruption. Callers may be students that want to get out of school early, someone who genuinely dislikes a student, staff member, or the district as a whole, or the threat could be legitimate. Every threat should be taken seriously.

In the spring semester of 2012, Adam Busby, the self-proclaimed leader of the Scottish National Liberation Army, e-mailed the University of Pittsburgh numerous times with bomb threats (Ove, 2015). In a single day, seventeen bomb threats were made. Over the course of the semester, 136 evacuations of on-campus facilities had occurred. By the end of the semester, university leadership had to restructure final exams and advise students of new final exam procedures.

One could only imagine how much disruption the aforementioned incident would cause. Students had to be evacuated many times during cold and inclement weather. Those evacuations disrupted classes, final exams, and sleep patterns. They also created a sense of fear. With every threat came the question of whether the threat was credible or plausible. According to *Pitt News* (2012), an independent student newspaper, during final exams, the university advised students that they were to remain in place during final exams unless otherwise told to evacuate. This was a judgment call that had to be made during a time when academic integrity must be sustained.

Though bomb threats are not necessarily preventable, mitigating from worsening situations after these threats is crucial. Knowing how to respond to a bomb threat and what to be prepared for will ultimately reduce the potential for confusion and furthering disruptions.

Anyone who answers a phone at your district or who greets visitors should be trained in your bomb threat protocols. Essentially, any administrative faculty and all leadership should be prepared to know what to do when a threat is made in any fashion of communication. A great start in bomb threat preparedness is to make a *Bomb Threat Checklist*, such as the one in figure 6.1.

This form can be as generic or complex as your school decides. It is your form, so make it so that your staff will be comfortable with it. Considering the potential frantic scenario that a bomb threat causes, it is best to keep it simple and readily accessible. Readily accessible does not mean tucked away in a file drawer. Readily accessible means it should be on your desk or at an arm's length away from your phone. The call-taker should not have to think about where their checklist is. It should be out in the open or on ready-to-go in a top drawer.

Bomb threat responses are at the discretion of each school. Whether your school decides to evacuate for every threat or to lockdown, know what the plan is. Having said that, consider the following scenario.

Scenario 6.1

One of the administrative assistants at your high school just answered a phone call and received a bomb threat. She has been well-trained in bomb threat scenarios, thanks to your new emergency management culture and training implementation. She tells you that the caller was young, sounded like a boy or a man, and he had a calm demeanor. Additionally, she said that she could hear lots of talking in the background.

FBI BOMB PROGRAM EBCC-X
BOMB THREAT CALL CHECKLIST

Questions to Ask   Exact Wording of the Threat:
1. When is bomb going to explode?   _____
2. Where is it right now?   _____
3. What does it look like?   _____
4. What kind of bomb is it?   _____
5. What will cause it to explode?   _____
6. Did you place the bomb?   _____
7. Why?   _____
8. What is your address?   _____
9. What is your name?

Sex of caller _____ Age _____ Race _____ Length of call _____

BOMB THREAT QUESTIONNAIRE:

CALLER'S VOICE:

___ Calm	___ Laughing	___ Lisp	___ Disguised
___ Angry	___ Crying	___ Raspy	___ Accent
___ Excited	___ Normal	___ Deep	___ Familiar
___ Slow	___ District	___ Ragged	___ If voice is familiar
___ Rapid	___ Slurred	___ Clearing throat	who did it sound like?
___ Soft	___ Nasal	___ Deep breathing	_____
___ Loud	___ Stutter	___ Cracking voice	

BACKGROUND SOUNDS:

___ Street noises	___ House noises	___ Factory	___ Local
___ Crockery	___ Motor	___ Machinery	___ Long distance
___ Voices	___ Office Machinery	___ Clear	___ Animal Noises
___ Booth	___ PA System	___ Static	___ Music

Other _____

THREAT LANGUAGE:

___ Well spoken (educated)	___ Foul	___ Incoherent
___ Irrational	___ Taped	___ Message read by threat maker

REMARKS
:
_____
_____

Report call immediately to _____ Phone number _____

Fill out completely, immediately after bomb threat   Date / /
Phone number
Name _____   Position _____

EBCC-X Bomb Threat Call Checklist

Figure 6.1. Owens Community College, 2017.

The caller said that there is a bomb sitting on a toilet in the boys' bathroom in the east wing of your school. He did not give any description of what the bomb looked like.

Given the information from your administrative assistant:

1. What is your plan?
2. Who do you notify?
3. Will you evacuate or stay in place while the incident is investigated?

Nobody can answer these questions but you and your school. It is important to remember not to get tunnel vision and to take every threat seriously. You may ask yourself, why would our school ever stay in place during a bomb threat? Remember that mitigation from worsening the situation is crucial. It is a tough decision to make, but you have to go with what information you have from the call taker.

If you evacuate, accountability of students is harder to maintain, and more importantly, the caller could be setting you up for a bigger attack. However, if you stay in place, students are still in the facility of where the threat is. The caller could have told you that the bomb was in the east wing, guessing that you would have to have more students go out other exits they normally would use, but in reality, the bomb could be in another place. The caller could also be setting you up to begin a shooting attack as students and staff exit the school.

Take every threat seriously and make a decision based on the information you have. Do not wait until a bomb threat happens to test your plans. Train your staff on what is expected of them in that situation. If everyone knows his or her roles, you are already setting your school up to be prepared.

PARENT–STUDENT REUNIFICATION

When it comes to emergency planning, parent reunification is one of the most important processes to plan for. This is one part of the plan that must be tailored to your school(s). Parent–student reunification is the process of reuniting students with their parent(s) or legal guardian(s). It is a process that can be very confusing and unsafe if it is not practiced and well coordinated.

If a school is initiating a parent–student reunification process, it typically means an emergency of some type has occurred and it is necessary to connect the students with their families in a safe manner. The parent–student reunification process can be as simple or as complex as your school would like. No matter what your plan is, make sure it is tested at least once a year.

Reunifications do not just have to be used for severe active situations like active shooters, they can also be used for school structural problems, utility issues, or poststorm events. Ideally, your school should use the risk assessment processes that were discussed in chapter 1 to decide which of those threats are most likely to cause an activation of the reunification process.

A parent–student reunification process should have following six components that must all be secure locations.

1. Parent/guardian entrance
2. Request room
3. Student staging room
4. Parent–student reunification area
5. A family grief room
6. A secure exit

To visualize a parent–student reunification process, refer to figure 6.2.

Philpott and Serluco (2009) originally described a similar movement through a parent reunification site. However, they only illustrated that a student holding room, a report point, and a release point be included in parent reunification. While that may be sufficient for smaller, more basic incidents, it is a better idea to have a parent reunification plan that is more specific and descriptive.

It does not matter if the school decides to use its own facility or an off-site facility as a reunification site. Just be sure that the facility is capable of having these six components. Having these six components will allow for an "assembly line"–type process that keeps the flow of foot traffic moving.

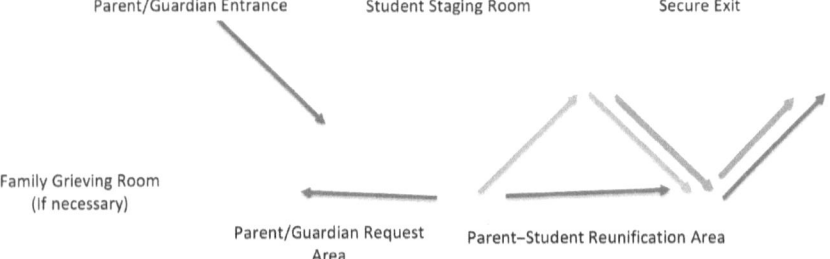

Figure 6.2.

The parent/guardian entrance is just as it sounds. The school should have staff members or signage guiding families to this area when they enter the facility. Encourage the use of volunteers of community emergency response teams and community civilians. During a time like this, the school will need all the help it can get. The entrance should be an entrance only. Nobody should go out these doors except for those who request a child and are denied. No children that have been reunited with their parent/guardian should leave through these doors.

The request room is also as it sounds. It is the location within the facility where parents and guardians request the reunification of their child/children. The request room is where school staff, preferably a BERT (see chapter 5), identifies who the person is that is requesting the child and whether he or she is listed as a person having permission to retrieve the child from the parent–student reunification. There are many ways of doing this, but the request always starts with who the recipient of the child is.

At the beginning of each school year, paperwork should be sent home with students to be brought to parents about who they will allow for the child to be picked up from school. It should be made aware to the parents that phone calls, e-mails, and texts from a parent to the school to allow a child to go home with someone who is not on the list is not acceptable. It is for the child's safety that this procedure is in place. Parents should also be required to have identification during the reunification process to prove they are who they say they are.

Your school should decide how this process should work. An example of this process could be that a BERT or staff member takes a picture on a tablet or phone. The device is then given to a runner, another staff member, to take to the child that is being requested. If the child positively identifies that the person is who he or she says he or she is, the process can continue. If he or she is not who he or she says he or she is, the process ends and that person has an explanation of why it is ending and is asked to leave.

After the child and staff have positively been identified, the runner should escort the parent to the parent–student reunification area. The runner should then escort them both to the exit and return to the request area for his or her next assignment.

The student holding area can either be a location where all students are reunified or it may just hold the students that were in an isolated incident. For instance, if a school bus accident occurred and the students who are uninjured are transported back to school, it may be a good idea to start a reunification specifically for those students. If there is potential for students to be in the holding location for a long period of time, be prepared to have board games, card games, charging outlets, and so on to keep the students occupied.

The family grief room is an important location to have as a part of your process. If a parent requests his or her child, but the staff knows they are asking about a student who is injured or deceased, that parent/guardian should be pulled aside to the grief room. Your BERT/staff members assisting in the reunification process should be well trained on how to handle parents that are grieving or upset. This is a sensitive situation and should be treated as such.

No information of the student's status should be given to the parent in the request area. The parent/guardian's emotions should be respected. The person receiving the request for the student victim should notify the supervisor running the reunification area and the appropriate district staff should softly break the news to the parent on the student's whereabouts and conditions. Allow the family member to take as much time as they need to gather themselves before leaving to go wherever the child is. It may be a good idea to have more than one room for families to grieve if there are many casualties.

This is where a properly equipped BERT would come in great assistance. School counselors can be used to help with various tasks until someone needs to grieve or just talk. School nurses can assess students as they enter the student holding area for any lingering injuries. Teachers and custodians can operate the request area and can act as runners. No matter how you plan for reunification, test it so that your staff can understand the atmosphere.

Other incidents to consider mitigating are topics like social media response, using law enforcement, injured and deceased student tracking, and having several reunification plans on-site and off-site.

More than likely when an emergency occurs, students will have posted about the emergency and their status before 911 is even dialed and responders arrive. The school should have a social media response that gives updated information on how parents can get in contact with their children.

The use of law enforcement is ideal for reunification. Discuss with your local police department on what your reunification plans are and how many officers it would take to create a safe atmosphere for your process. At least one police officer should be at the entrance and another one should be at the exit.

For security purposes, you may want to share with them where all of your potential reunification facilities are. Be sure to tour the off-site facilities if you plan on using them. It would be a logistics nightmare if the school told the parents that reunification is going to take place at a local fire company where another major event is currently going on.

Additionally, students that have gone to the hospital or are deceased should be tracked so that there is no confusion when parents arrive to reunite with their child. If possible, have the names of the students and which hospital they are in. Keep a separate list of the deceased children.

Parent–student reunification can be a complex plan. Do not wait to throw shots in the dark when an emergency occurs. If you wait until then, your staff will be unprepared, which will cause chaos. The process may not be simple, but the day the emergency occurs, your preparedness will be much better and could make the process much simpler.

IMPLEMENT A BULLYING PROGRAM

According to a 2014 study by researchers at Cohen Children's Medical Center of New York, students who are bullied are twice as likely to bring a weapon to school (Adesman & Shapiro, 2014). Knowing that, how differently will you treat bullying situations? Though bullying can happen anywhere, typically it breeds in schools where peer pressure is almost ubiquitous.

Like your active shooter program, the entire school or school district should be on the same page about bullying. Students should also be educated in bullying because they may be bullying someone and not even know it. Having students identifying themselves as a bully or having bullied someone could be your first line of defense.

When a student, parent, or staff member reports bullying, take it seriously. The ramifications of giving it less attention than you think it needs could be deadly. If parents know, or even think they know, that their child is being bullied, they just want to see that something is done about it. The last thing you want is a parent or victim of the bullying feeling as though he or she needs to take matters into his or her own hands.

Find a bullying program that works for your school and add it into your culture. Make it an everyday conversation past the point of nauseum. Will people get tired of hearing about bullying? Probably. If you make your stance clear and enforce your policies, you will create the kind and responsive school climate you are looking for, but remember that *it* starts at the top.

PREPARING FOR STUDENTS WITH SPECIAL NEEDS (SANTIAGO, 2017)

No matter how large or small your special needs community may be within your school, it is always best to be prepared for emergencies. Students with special needs may need extra assistance during an emergency. When planning for these students, it is critical that you have your special needs staff members involved. They know and understand their students' abilities better than anyone. They can give you great insight on how best to prepare these students, their teachers, and their classrooms for an emergency.

Firstly, you have to know for whom you are preparing. You will need to have an exact number of how many students use wheelchairs and power chairs, how many cannot see, how many cannot hear, and so forth. If there are twenty students in your school who are legally deaf, you may need more assistance from staff during an emergency to control the chaos.

Next, it is a good idea to have a buddy system. Put students with someone that they get along with well and who they trust. Having someone to rely on and look out for is a best practice. Buddy systems also allow for distraction from the overall emergency. Be sure to use the buddy system in all types of drills to make sure that it works for the class and that the buddies are correctly paired.

Schools should also include the parents when planning for students with special needs. Discuss with each individual set of parents how they think their child would react during certain situations. Including the parents not only benefits you and the students but also gains their trust because you are considering their child.

You should know what medications your students are taking and how a missed dosage would affect them. For instance, if a school is on lockdown, but a student is due for insulin, it may create another incident inside of your already existing incident. Mitigate that potential additional medical emergency by communicating with administrators and school nurses during the incident and also know what to expect when a student misses his or her dosage.

Finally, have a go-bag. The bag should have whatever you think is necessary so that the students can remain healthy and calm during an incident. They may be forced to shelter-in-place for hours at a time, be prepared ahead of time by creating a go-bag. Ideal items to have in your go-bag include, but are not limited to, the following:

- Whistles
- Tissues
- Bottles of water
- Batteries
- Phone chargers
- Hand tools (screw drivers, pliers, etc.)
- First-aid kit
- Small ice chest for medications
- Protein bars
- Attendance sheets with parental/guardian contact information
- A flipchart emergency plan/procedures manual
- Noise canceling headphones
- Fidget toys to keep students' minds off the incident
- Weighted blankets

CHAPTER 6 SUMMARY

Do not limit your preparedness to these scenarios. Use your risk assessment to identify where your vulnerabilities are. Remember that you cannot prepare for every possible situation so it is best to have a plan that fits multiple scenarios. Whatever your plan is, just be sure that everyone will be on the same page.

Use your staff. They are more capable than you think. If you train them how you would like them to respond, they will know what you expect of them. They will also know what the steps are through each phase of an emergency.

Above all else, prepare. It is not a matter of if these scenarios can happen, it is a matter of when.

CHAPTER 6 PERSONAL INVENTORY

1) What types of situations do you feel your school is most prepared for?
2) What types of situations do you feel your school is least prepared for?
3) Consider the climate of your school's emergency preparedness culture. How would you rate it from 1 to 10, if 10 is the best and that nothing could be changed?
4) Has your school considered preparing for students with special needs?
5) What laws are in your state regarding school emergency planning?
   a. Do you meet the law?
   b. Do you do more than what is required by the law?

Chapter Seven

Special Events at Your School

> Plan for what is difficult while it is easy, do what is great while it is easy.
>
> —Sun Tzu,
> Chinese military strategist, writer, philosopher

At the conclusion of chapter 7, readers will be able to:

- Consider the spectrum of events that your school hosts that can be dangerous
- Identify what security measures to implement to create a safer atmosphere
- Identify what personnel will be needed for safety and security measures

It is troubling enough to know that during a normal school day, your school is a soft target. Now your school will be hosting a major event that will bring thousands of visitors from all over the region. There will be food trucks there, parking will be a potential issue, and it will take a large amount of people for this event to go well. You would hope there would be no issues, but it is impossible to know what someone may do or what act of the universe could occur.

It may be financially rewarding to host major high school and youth sporting events or even a regional event in your auditorium. Have you considered the ramification of what would happen if an emergency were to occur at or near your event? Is there a plan in place? Most schools will answer with some type of a "no" response. Even if your event has nothing to do with academics or interscholastic extracurricular events, if an emergency occurs on your school grounds, it is now your problem as an administrator.

Planning should begin well in advance for major events. As an administrator, you are probably aware of the events that are typically held annually at your school. Occasionally, you might host a large event that is out of the ordinary. Either way, if your school is hosting an event, it is ideal to meet with all the stakeholders well in advance to discuss not only operations and timelines but also safety and security.

Outside events are particularly difficult to plan for because the space where people can move and roam is probably endless. It would be a good idea to include school security, if you have it, and local police to sit in on the meetings that take place regarding your events. With outside events, there is potential for vendors of all kinds. There will also be sensitive areas where the general public should and should not be. If your school is not considering these components of major events, it should be.

PHYSICAL SECURITY

Physical security is the foundation of any event. It is anything that is tangible that can protect people. Examples of physical security would be fencing, jersey barriers, gates, checkpoints, bollards, and so forth. Maintaining physical security at your events is critical because it will help control vehicular and foot traffic, and you can layer security around your event.

Fencing and signs are very helpful for people who are unfamiliar with your facility. Fencing and signage also prevent people from wandering in places where they should not be. They may simply be trying to get to their destination, but because of lack of traffic guidance with fencing and signage, they end up where they should not be. Signage can also play a security factor by letting people know what is acceptable and what is not. If you do not want spectators standing near an entrance, that area probably deserves some signs to let people know that you do not want them standing there.

Checkpoints can play a similar role at events as well. A good use of several check points will allow people to continue to gain access to their destination. For instance, the first checkpoint may be where people purchase their tickets. After they purchase their ticket, they continue on to the next checkpoint where there may be a security measure of some type. After they pass, the security feature is probably where they hand the ticket to a staff member so that they are allowed in the event. Deciding on one that works for you is critical to your event operation. Be careful not to add features that will cause unnecessary vehicular or foot traffic.

OPERATIONAL SECURITY

Operational security is the security plan you have in place and distribute it to the people who need to know what the plan is. There may be sensitive parts to your security plan that the general public should not know so that you can maintain the security of your event. If there is a secretive communications area that people should not know about, unnecessary people or the public should not be told about it. Out of sight, out of mind.

Another integral part of operational security is timelines. If a timeline is set from start to finish of what will be happening, who will be doing it, and when, that information should be considered sensitive and should not be disseminated to people who do not need to know.

BACKGROUND SECURITY

Background security is only important for school events if your school decides to contract services during an event. Food vendors and security companies are great examples of common contracted services during school events. Ideally, the school should have a background check of all persons working for the vendor at the event, as well as the company itself.

Threats can be mitigated through the use of background security. If you know that someone working for a french fry vendor at the next school event is a convicted child molester, it is probably a good idea to not have him or her work at your school event. Same as if that same french fry vendor has gotten people sick in the past or has had poor inspection reports, you probably do not want him or her serving food at your event.

Many times, background checks are not an issue for companies to conduct on their employees. However, stopping someone with a bad history from working at your event could save your school's event.

Scenario 7.1

Your school's high school soccer field has just won a bid to hold the state soccer finals for all high school levels at a year from now. The event will host six games in one day. The first game will begin at 9 a.m. and the last game will be held at 8 p.m. In recent years, 20,000 spectators have come throughout the day to watch the championship games.

Food and security vendors have already been contacting your school trying to get in on the consumers at the games. Given the number of spectators, you will probably run out of parking at your facility.

Scenario 7.1 Questions

1) When should your planning begin?
2) How often should you meet?
3) Who should be included in the planning?
4) What physical security measures will you have in place?
5) What operational security measures will you have in place?
6) How much security will you need?
7) Will background checks need to be conducted? If so, on who?

These are only a few questions that will need to be answered. Surely, thousands more will need to be answered as plans are set. Once timelines are put together, how do you protect them from being released? For instance, if you know that twelve teams are playing at your field, you will need to know what time they are arriving and where the buses will be staged. For someone trying to do harm at your event, that could be very helpful information of when and where he or she would do his or her attack and how.

CREDENTIALING

Knowing who is involved on your staff is an important operational security measure. If you have security companies or many staff members that you may not know working at your event, you do not want to have to do an on-site background check on who they are. Staff and spectators should immediately know who the event staff are in case there is a problem.

With that being said, an event that lasts a few days like sporting events or conferences may become dangerous. Credentialing is the process of identifying who is working at your event as a staff member. The staff member should have some type of badge on a lanyard or a shirt that proves who he or she is. Credentialing is another procedure that can be as simple or as complex as you want it to be.

If there is an event that lasts a few days, you may want to consider using different colored shirts or badges for each day for your staff. This process makes it difficult for staff impersonators to create a shirt or a badge. As a part of operational security, for those who do not need to know the colors and designs of the shirts or badges for each day, do not share that information with those people. If that information gets to the wrong person, it is just another process that makes it easier for an unauthorized person to work in an area that is sensitive to a safe, successful event.

Another important component to consider with events is if you only want certain staff members to be authorized in certain areas or facilities. An example of this would be if you did not want members of a private security company in the locker rooms or in the press box. Those areas should require different credentialing. However, someone must be posted at each of those sensitive locations to check for correct credentialing.

Simply put, credentialing allows for staff members to easily recognize whether someone is allowed to be where he or she is and doing what he or she is doing. If credentialing is done correctly, it can be, and should be, a huge part of your school hosting major events.

CHAPTER 7 SUMMARY

Special events at schools are inevitable. Schools need to hold events and sometimes host major events for external organizations. Though these events may not be a part of the school organization, if an emergency occurs, it becomes the school's problem.

Events can be so wide open and have no organization to them whatsoever. However, the more you plan and take pride in your ability to host events, the better prepared you will be when something happens during an event. Consider the three facets of security (physical, operational, and background) when planning for you events. Determine what your biggest vulnerabilities are and how you can harden your position as a soft target.

CHAPTER 7 PERSONAL INVENTORY

1) What special events does your school host regularly?
2) What major events has your school hosted in the past?
   a. What went well?
   b. What could have been better?
3) Do your administrators know and understand the three facets of security?
4) Does your school currently have any credentialing processes for special events?

Chapter Eight

School Transportation

There is no harm in hoping for the best as long as you're prepared for the worst.

—Stephen King,
Different Seasons, American author

At the conclusion of chapter 8, readers will be able to:

- Identify risk management techniques for student transportation
- Understand the importance of driver hiring, training, and policies
- Understand the importance of preparing for emergencies when transporting students

For most schools, transporting students is a necessity. Unless your school is an inner city school, the transportation of your students is probably a sizable operation. Your school may not even be responsible for the student transportation operation. Maybe your school hires a contractor or maybe your state is in charge of the school bus operation.

Nevertheless, the school is responsible for the safety of the children. Even though a school district representative may not be on the buses while students are transported, parents will look to the school for answers if their child comes within the cross hairs of harm's way. It is the school's responsibility to reassure parents that coordination between the school and the contractor or state organization has occurred and that plans are in place for emergencies.

INTERNAL STUDENT TRANSPORTATION OPERATION

If your school or district owns its buses, maintains those buses, and hires the drivers, the cards are in your favor. The reason this is a good thing is because it is an operation that your school or district can control. Your school can hire its own drivers, decide on student transportation policies, and essentially manage your operation. This operation should be treated no differently in regard to risk management or emergency preparedness. There should be policies in place for both risk management and emergency response of the district.

While it may seem like a good thing to have this operation in complete and total control, there are downside risks to having and operating a student transportation system. All of the risk is on your school and your school's insurance carrier, if you have one. There is no risk to transfer or share because the school is both the organization in need of the transportation system and the provider of the transportation system. That is one of many obvious reasons why it is in your school's best interest to properly manage the operation and prepare for risks whether they are preventable or not.

CONTRACTOR-HIRED STUDENT TRANSPORTATION OPERATION

If your school has a contract with a company that provides student transportation for the district, this lightens the load of the risk on the school, but it does not mean you can completely be hands-off with its operation. Even if your school has a great relationship with the transportation contractor, district officials should not just "believe" the contractor is doing its job, they should be sure of it. A good relationship, to some, may seem like the district should just allow the contractor to conduct its operations; however, the school should be involved in much of the planning and coordination process.

Having an external contractor provide transportation does allow for a risk transfer or a shareable risk, but when an accident occurs, parents will surely be calling the school for answers. It is a best practice to create emergency response plans *with* the contractor so that both organizations can coordinate an effort for emergency purposes.

Scenario 8.1

You are a top administrator at your school. You have just received a call from your point of contact at the bus company that one of your school's buses has been involved in an accident. There are no details on if there are any casualties. The only detail you know is where the crash has occurred.

Parents are beginning to call your school because they have seen social media posts from students on the bus, and some students have even called their parents to come pick them up from the scene.

What do you do?

It would be a bad day to make this situation worse by not having any plans, and if you do have plans, never having practiced them. This situation could go one of three ways.

1. Neither personnel from the contracted company nor the school show up to the accident scene because they each assumed the other would be there.
2. Too many people from both organizations show up and now nobody is able to coordinate response and recovery efforts.
3. Both organizations respond appropriately and the district and the contractor quickly manage the situation. A timely media statement has also been made.

Number three on the list is clearly the most desired outcome. However, emergency responses from both organizations will not just *happen* to turn out that way. Without proper plans, cocoordination, and exercising those plans, more than likely the situation's outcome will be closer to numbers one or two.

HIRING DRIVERS

The hiring of the drivers that will be responsible for the safe transportation of your school's students is pretty important. Students who use the school's transportation system will likely start and end each of their school days on a bus. Choosing the right people for this job can be challenging, but you must not settle. The safety and well-being of your students does not begin and end at your school buildings. Their safety and well-being starts and ends on their way to school and on their way home from school. Driving a student transportation vehicle is important, do not ever let your drivers feel otherwise.

Hiring drivers for your district should be a coordinated effort. That could mean a few different approaches depending on whether or not your district has an internal system or a contracted system. If the state runs your bus system, there may be limited opportunity for you to be involved with hiring, but try anyway.

If your school has an internal operation, the cards are in your favor again because you get to choose the drivers internally. There still should be a coordinated effort of who decides on who is hired. Just as your school would hire a teacher, your school probably does not allow for one single person to do the hiring and interviewing. More than likely, your school has a panel or a committee that interviews and decides on who should be hired. Use that to your advantage by setting standards for drivers you would like to hire.

If your school uses a contractor for your transportation services, make an agreement in the contract that says which personnel from your school will be required in each part of the hiring process. This shows the parents that you are involved and a representative from the school is involved with who is hired. It also sends a message to the contractor that your school will be involved and there will be oversight. At the end of the day, your school is responsible for its students, whether a child is hurt on school property or on a bus.

Hiring standards should be set for all drivers. Things like acceptable traffic citations, if any, and how many should be established. Acceptable criminal records are another element to discuss. If a person who had a misdemeanor drug charge twenty years ago passed all your hiring tests outstandingly, would your school hire him or her? Some would say yes, others would not even consider him or her. Set your standards and stick to them to avoid discrimination suits from those who are not hired. Consistency is key.

TRANSPORTATION RISK MANAGEMENT

This section is another section where it is a good idea to find out what the laws are in your state. Some states are really strict when it comes to student transportation. In one state, your bus may not be legally allowed to go into another state or territory without proper licensing or permitting. Other states are more lenient. Be sure to check what is required of your school bus operation.

Once you find what is required by your state's laws, go beyond the law and make an even safer environment if you can. Whatever you do, do not cut corners or *bend* these laws, your school will get burned eventually. Do more than what is required.

No matter what the laws are, research school transportation best practices. Talk with your insurance agent or carrier to find out what processes and procedures they would like to see in order to prevent or mitigate any risks. Your aim is to have zero accidents and zero injuries. Create an environment that can do that for your school.

There are many types of risk management techniques in school transportation systems. Examples of these techniques are as follows:

1. Pre- and post-trip inspections by your drivers. Drivers should be required to fill out daily paperwork before they make any trips and after they return. There are a few reasons this is a best practice. First, it documents if the

bus is OK to drive and it allows drivers to document any problems with the bus. These forms can then be used to track maintenance and recall problems at a later time. This process also should require drivers to check all bus seats upon return in case a child remains on the bus and is not left on a locked bus overnight.
2. Safety talks should be conducted at least weekly, but should actually occur daily. Make safety the number one priority and talk about it at nauseum. Your drivers may get tired of talking about safety, but they will not forget it if it is prioritized.
3. Implement policies to prevent accidents, then enforce them. Policies should be created for instances like backing up a school transportation vehicle, texting and driving, and accident procedures. Having all of these policies, and any others your school feels necessary, will create a standard that will mitigate risks by themselves. When there comes a time where a driver violates one or more of these policies, the district or the contractor should handle the situation appropriately. Accidents happen, and maybe someone should not be fired for an accident. But if accidents continue to occur, or controlled substances are involved, it may call for termination. Create policies, then enforce them with consistency.
4. Have a driver orientation. Just because a school hires a driver that has twenty years of experience without an accident does not mean he or she put safety first. It could be that the person has been fortunate that nothing has happened. All drivers that are new to your school should have an orientation that lasts a week or longer. This orientation process allows for you to reiterate your policy priorities and exercise your plans.

Again, these techniques are only a few of many that your school can coordinate or implement. Create a standard, reiterate it, and enforce it. If your school has incurred losses in student transportation, implementing policies and giving remedial training on expectations to drivers is a great technique as well. Remember the goal, zero accidents and zero injuries.

STUDENT TRANSPORTATION EMERGENCY PREPAREDNESS

Preparing for transportation emergencies should be conducted just as you would prepare for any other emergency. Through a risk assessment, determine what vulnerabilities your transportation system has and then decide what is most likely to happen to your school bus system. Because school bus accidents or losses typically occur away from school property, these emergencies will require you and your committee to think outside the box.

School bus accidents are commonly the most thought of emergency for schools, and reasonably so. The transportation system is used daily throughout the school year. Not only are these buses driven many miles for many hours but they are also driven through harsh weather like heavy rain, wind, snow, ice, and dust. Miles and hours of operation alone will cause wear and tear on a bus. Add in earth's elements and the lifespan of a bus is greatly shortened. On top of that, if buses are not properly maintained, they can become dangerous to drive, which puts your students in danger.

If accidents are largely a concern among your emergency planning committee, plan for your operation. If your transportation operation is run solely by your school, determine what should happen when an accident occurs. The same should be done if your school hires a contractor to provide transportation services, but your planning efforts should include the contractor.

It is easiest if the planners map out how exactly a response to an accident will occur. First, there is the accident. Who should the driver call to notify responders of the accident? Some schools want the driver to call his or her supervisor, who then calls 911, and others want the drivers themselves to call 911. It is at the discretion of the school, just make sure that the drivers know what is expected of them.

After 911 is notified, representatives from the school, and, if applicable, personnel from the contractor should both respond. Determine who should stay behind to keep school operations running and also be neutralized from the scene. It is not a good idea to send all top-level administrators to the scene.

Typically, an administrator and the person who is in charge of the district's transportation respond directly to the scene. Another person to have on scene is an experienced school bus mechanic. A mechanic is useful to first responders to advise them of what precautions need to be taken in order to maintain a safe response effort. The mechanic will also be able to determine if the bus is able to be driven wherever necessary or if it will need to be towed.

If there are injuries and students are transported to the hospital, how will you track them? Work with local hospital personnel and emergency responders to determine the best way to track deceased and injured students.

Now that you have determined how to track the injured students, what will be done with the uninjured students? Where will they go and how will they get there? Anything can happen in an emergency, do not worsen the situation by keeping the uninjured students on scene for longer than necessary. The uninjured students may already be grieving the gruesome injury or loss of a friend, and keeping them on scene for them to see more than they need to is not healthy. Removing the uninjured students from the scene also prevents them from being injured from other traffic.

Accidents will happen, and many of them will never go how you think they would go. Be prepared to adapt to the incident and think quickly. Students will be posting to social media, parents will be calling the school, and other parents will show up directly to the scene. Prepare your staff to overcome difficult situations and identify what your expectations for them are.

Other situations your school may need to prepare for are what to do with your buses during extreme weather. For instance, if the location where you keep your buses is in a flood plain, what do you plan on doing with them during a major rain storm? If you keep them there, you and your insurance carrier will face a huge loss. If you plan on moving them, determine where they should be moved to and how you plan on doing it. If residents are told to evacuate and the drivers follow the government's orders to evacuate, how will the buses get moved? Do not spare any potential threats to your bus system. Anything can happen. If you are prepared, more than likely you can mitigate the situation from worsening.

CHAPTER 8 SUMMARY

The process for planning for transportation emergencies should be no different. Though the scenarios may be different, the process that you use to plan should not be. Transportation emergencies can be tricky. Do not wait for an emergency to occur before testing your emergency plans.

Take the time to coordinate with your transportation contractor, if you have one. Decide on things like who should be involved with the hiring process, who should go to the scene during an emergency, and so forth. Saving time on the front end of an emergency will certainly save time on the back end of an emergency.

Implement risk management techniques into your transportation operation. Mitigating losses or controlling current ones will save your school money and will prevent injuries and accidents. Policies alone are not enough to control risks. If policies are not enforced after implementation, they are useless. Consistently enforce your policies and let it be known that nobody is above following the rules and the law.

CHAPTER 8 PERSONAL INVENTORY

1) What type of school bus operation does your school have? State run, internal, or contracted?
2) Does your school have emergency plans in place?
   a. If so, do the personnel involved in the plan know their role?
   b. Have they been coordinated with the contractor, if your school has one?

3) Has the plan ever been tested?
4) What types of risk management techniques does your current transportation operation have?
5) Has your school ever had a school bus accident or emergency?
   a. What went well?
   b. What could be improved for the next accident?

Chapter Nine

Crisis Management

Don't wait until you are in a crisis to come up with a plan.

—Dr. Phil McGraw,
TV personality and psychologist

At the conclusion of chapter 9, readers will be able to:

- Understand how to use the media
- Create a crisis management team
- Manage a crisis
- Understand what an emergency operations center is

The majority of this book has been written to help schools prepare for the tangible loss in a school. Whether that means there were casualties after a major storm and the building was damaged or the school's petty cash was stolen, this book has mainly focused on the tangible losses. But what happens when something like a school's positive reputation is lost?

For instance, what if your superintendent was charged with drunk driving? Who decides what happens to him or her? Parents, taxpayers, and the media will want answers and if you do not have them in a timely manner, all three of those groups will work together until answers are given.

Everyone makes mistakes, we are all human. However, our negative actions have consequences. Emergency preparedness is not just about preparing for emergencies. All emergencies start with some type of risk management or crisis management. Though there are always inevitable acts of the universe, measures can be taken to mitigate those threats.

Crises can arise at any moment with any organization. However, the microscope is definitely more focused on government and public organizations where people pay taxes. They have a right to know where their money is going and why. So, when you decide to keep your superintendent on staff as if nothing happened after he or she was charged with drunk driving, you better have an answer. The same goes for if you decide to terminate him or her.

Crises will happen to everyone. However, typically, it is not only the crisis that can be damaging. The response of the agency to the crisis can also worsen the crisis. A good response, however, can repair the image of the organization and maintain relationships that could have been lost in the process.

A good way to manage accidents and crises is to create a crisis management team (CMT). CMTs operate similarly to a safety committee and can actually operate as both if you wanted it to. Safety committees usually only review vehicular and workplace accidents. While it is a great practice to have a safety committee, why not have a group of people that have the authority to respond to these accidents instead of just forwarding their findings to the school board directors?

If a person who is a part of the custodial staff has had a history of accidents while driving district vehicles and he or she is never reprimanded, what happens when he or she strikes a pedestrian with a school vehicle? More than likely the public is going to want to know why he or she was still able to drive without any conversations or remedial training. The CMT not only should have the ability to review the accident, but they should also be authorized to distribute a press release with an appropriate message about the accident.

CMTs should not just be school district leaders making decisions. CMTs should be made up of different levels of employees from the district that are in different roles. There are a few reasons for this. First, school district leaders may think that a group of staff are doing what they are supposed to be doing, but if a person from that group of staff is on the CMT, they may be able to shed some truths to the rest of the CMT about what *really* happens. Also, if someone from the mid-level of staff is on the CMT, they may become an enforcer of the rules because they were included on the CMT. They would know that if something went wrong and they knew about it and did not report that incident to the CMT, they could be reprimanded.

Inclusion of all levels of employees is important because it creates buy in. When you get buy in from all levels of employees on a risk management practice, you will more than likely create a better risk culture and a safer school atmosphere. A culture will be created where if someone makes a poor decision, he or she will be held accountable for that decision. With that in mind, you cannot bring the hammer down on someone for his or her first "minor" incident, whatever that may be. There must be a remediation process that allows for problems to be fixed and not always just punish one of your staff members.

The crisis management team should also be educated in how to properly manage the media. The media can either hurt you or help you. Your responses to them will determine how they choose to portray you during their segments. There are three simple rules when it comes to working with the media:

1) Be Honest
   Telling lies, half-truths, or manipulation of the truth will only hurt your relationship with the media. If you do not know an answer to their question, tell them that. If you know the answer, but cannot tell them the answer, then tell them you cannot answer the question at this time. Be honest.
2) Tell Them What They *NEED* to Know
   The media deserve to know the truth so they can share that information with the public, your taxpayers. However, they do not need to know every single detail. You can get yourself in trouble by providing too much information. Keep it simple, keep it brief, keep it honest.
3) Set Timelines
   Setting timelines for the media about when you will release additional information is critically important, especially during a situation that is ongoing. By setting timelines with the media about the next release of information, it creates a trust factor between you and them. Without timelines, the potential is created for the media to come up with their own stories if you are not able to give them the information they are looking for in a timely manner.

EMERGENCY OPERATIONS CENTERS

Emergency operations centers (EOCs) are facilities that are at a neutral location from an incident where coordination between multiple agencies can occur. Often times, EOCs can be referred to as MACCs or Multi-Agency Coordination Centers. MACCs and EOCs allow persons with authority from single or multiple agencies to coordinate an event or emergency. EOCs and MACCs can make communication smoother and allows for overall monitoring of an event or an emergency.

For major events or incidents, it may be a good idea for a school to have its own EOC. Leaders, department heads, and top-level administrators should be included in your EOC. If it is an expanding incident, you may want to consider bringing in a person from all of the agencies involved.

For instance, if there is an active shooter situation at an elementary school, it may be a good idea to start an EOC at a neutral location, like your administration building or maybe even the first responders have their own EOC. Large and expanding incidents can cause major miscommunications that could cost time and lives. EOCs will allow for decision-makers to get together and manage a situation away from the chaos of the emergency scene. It may sound strange to take the top decision-makers away from the incident, but if your people are well trained and trusted, there are other administrators that can be on scene communicating the directions you and the EOC are giving.

EOCs and MACCs should be held at facilities that can be survivable and self-sustaining for at least seventy-two hours and considerably up to two weeks (FEMA, EOC Management and Operations, 2008). These facilities should be incident-neutral and away from any chaotic conditions. Quiet, secure locations are best because decision-makers can easily think about what needs to happen without distraction.

Consider technology needs. How many computers, TVs, radios, landline phones, cell phone chargers, USB drives, and so forth will you need? Is there back-up power to support your operation after the loss of electricity? Consider the amount of people that will be in your EOC and determine your technology needs and what will suffice. Also consider the furniture you will need. How many tables and chairs will you need? Are there restrooms close by within the facility? Is there access to a break room or kitchen? Remember that you are trying to create a facility that will be survivable and self-sustaining.

Your EOC or MACC should not require much assembly. Your facility should always be set up and ready to go for an emergency. Taking the time to assemble the EOC could take an entire business day or more, your EOC could never effectively and efficiently be used if it is not ready to go when you get there. Consider the amount of space you will need. Make sure there is enough room so that people can walk behind chairs and not bump into others constantly.

It is a good idea to create a safety and security plan for your EOC or MACC. The last thing you want is for a situation to worsen because your EOC or MACC was not secure and now all of your decision-makers are dead because someone came into the facility and shot them. Create a security plan so that visitors and unauthorized personnel cannot easily access your EOC or MACC. Maintain its operational security by keeping the EOC as secretive as possible. The school should not announce where the EOC's or MACC's specific location is. Its location can be easily compromised if that is done.

Finally, test your EOC operation. Randomly activate your EOC during a normal school day and see who shows up. If an EOC or a MACC is a part of your EOP, then prioritize its use and make sure that the school administrators fully support its mission success. Do not just test who shows up. Also test your technology and its readiness. If possible, shut off the electricity to the facility and see if the back-up power is enough to sustain operations within your EOC.

CHAPTER 9 SUMMARY

Crises can and will happen to your school. They may occur in different magnitudes, but more than likely your school will be forced to respond. How they respond determines whether the damage that has already been done by the crisis can be repaired.

Create a CMT and include different levels of employees. Their input to your school's operation could prove to be incredibly invaluable. Use their information and their relationships with their coworkers to create a safe-minded environment so you can mitigate the chances of an accident occurring within the operation of your school.

CHAPTER 9 PERSONAL INVENTORY

1) Has your school ever experienced a major crisis?
    a. If so, how did your school respond?
    b. How could they have responded better?
2) Does your school have a safety committee or CMT?
    a. If so, what are their abilities?
    b. If not, would your school be receptive to having one?
    c. Who would you ask in order to start one?

Chapter Ten

Testing Your Plans

A good plan today is better than a perfect plan tomorrow.

—George S. Patton,
U.S. army general

At the conclusion of chapter 10, readers will be able to:

- Explain what types of exercises exist to test emergency plans
- Create their own exercises for their schools
- Properly use administrative/in-service days for emergency preparedness

At this phase in the emergency preparedness cycle, you should have completed your emergency plans. This is where most schools and organizations come to a screeching halt in the emergency preparedness process. Once the plan is complete, it is either bound nicely or put into a binder, distributed to all staff, and is never looked at again. While that nice bible of plans may look pretty, it will not save you any time, money, or lives if people do not know what is in it. The time to sort through those plans is not when you encounter an emergency.

Your emergency preparedness culture within your staff should already know what their role is during different types of emergencies. The only reasons that you put the plan on paper and into that nice binder is so that the Basic Plan shows that the district or school has agreed to the emergency plan that has been presented and also for legal purposes. When an emergency occurs, you will not be able to go line by line on what to do. There will be no time for that. In fact, that composition of plans more than likely will not even cross your mind during an emergency.

When an emergency occurs, you mind will be racing so quickly on what needs to be done, that if you have not already trained on what you should be doing, you are wasting time trying to figure out what needs to be done. That is why it is so important to practice what is in the binder to see if your plans work. Exercises give your school an opportunity to identify successes and areas of improvement within your plans so that you can change them, not so someone gets reprimanded for not doing the right thing. Exercises are simply about learning.

There are several different types of exercises that have different purposes that can all test your plans. The reasoning for the different types of exercises is because some cost a lot of money and time to coordinate and others are less involved but still very effective. All types of exercises should be used, but if they are not done correctly or in the right order, they more than likely will not be as effective as they could be.

Let's say that your school feels as though its emergency plans are complete. The school board of directors approves it and it is officially in effect. Administrators would now like to test parts of the plan, but they do not know where to begin. The first decision that needs to be made is whether the district will hire a consultant to aid in the exercise planning process. This process can be very overwhelming, and there are some great exercise-specific consultants out there. Keep in mind, however, that with great expertise comes a not-so-great price tag.

If your taxpayers and your school board decide that it is in the best interest to spend the money to have a professional test your plans, then great. Just know that your school does not have to go that route, though it is ideal to bring in experts for certain parts of your planning process. Learn to be resourceful. Challenge your employees and members of the emergency planning committee to learn more about school emergency preparedness on their own.

Next, let's say that the school district decided that it would not be in the school's or the taxpayer's best interest to hire a contractor because of the price tag that was proposed. The district now needs to know where to start testing their plans. Many times, schools want to jump right into a full-scale exercise where you bring in real first responders with real guns and real gurneys and paint up the actors to make them look bloody and injured. While that sounds fun and intriguing, that is not always the best place to start. In fact, if your school is new to emergency planning you should not start with a full-scale exercise.

WORKSHOP

Your newly adopted emergency plan is waiting to be unveiled to its potential users. Take the opportunity to do a workshop to not only unveil the plan but to have mini exercises too! Workshops are an opportunity to review plans, small pieces at a time. Do not plan on going over the whole plan in one sitting in its entirety. First of all, you will lose the attention of your audience, especially if whoever is presenting is not necessarily good at presenting. It is also not efficient to try to go over an entire emergency plan. Go over small parts at a time and touch on the most important parts.

After you introduce your staff to a part of the plan, test them. Have members of the emergency planning committee at the workshop break the group of staff up into smaller groups. Give them a one-page copy of the plan that was reviewed, so that everyone has the plan that is being tested in front of them, along with a scenario.

Allow the group to work through the scenario and let them play in roles that they normally may not be in. For example, allow a custodian to be an IC. He or she may not ever be the IC, but at least he or she will know how the plan and the emergency will go in that role.

Workshops allow for minimal confusion and are a learning environment given that the plans are new. Make this unveiling fun and try to earn as much buy in as possible.

TABLETOP EXERCISES

Tabletop exercises are the next useful step. A tabletop exercise is when a group of stakeholders sits around a table and works through a given scenario with a facilitator. The facilitator phrases questions to different people to see if the group can find any vulnerabilities in their plan. Tabletops can be anywhere from two to forty people. Any tabletop bigger than that will become inefficient and will likely not get everyone necessary involved.

There are two types of tabletop exercises that you can conduct. There are internal and combination tabletop exercises that serve similar, yet different, purposes. Internal tabletops are for only one organization. A group of various people in different positions from your school or district would sit at a table and will be given a scenario. The facilitator will ask the different roles what they would be doing in different phases of the incident. The group members will respond according to what they have learned from their emergency plans.

The facilitator should be assisted by an evaluator. The evaluator is the scribe. The evaluator also makes note on decisions that are made to identify later if those decisions follow the emergency plans and if there were any miscommunications of the plan. The evaluator exists so that the plans can be changed after vulnerabilities in the plan are identified.

Tabletop exercises are another great example of an atmosphere that has the ability to control the chaos. Yes, the room atmosphere can get hectic, given the emergency incident climate presented by the facilitator, but nobody is *actually* hurt and nothing is *actually* damaged. It allows the group to make decisions without being put down because an incident did not go well. It gives the group the opportunity to discuss where they can improve and what worked well.

After the group gets experience in participating in internal tabletops, the facilitator can then use variables that are likely to happen but could cause disruption. An example of a variable would be an emergency occurring and the building principal or the superintendent is out of town or if ten teachers came down with a food illness at school. There are endless amounts of variables for any situation. Just be sure that the variables are realistic.

Now that your school has been through an internal tabletop exercise, it is time to bring in external stakeholders to sit at the table. Those stakeholders may be first responders, local hardware stores, social workers, and so on. The point of this is to help your school staff realize that how they believe an emergency will go, it probably will not, and how they believe the stakeholders should respond, and how they may not.

When the group comes to a moment when it realizes that something will not go as they thought it would, it is a good idea to stop the exercise and work through that scenario until the group agrees on how it should go. For instance, the school may think that if they need to request ten buses from their bus company at any time of day. The busing company may look at them and say, "We do have other operations to provide for, you know." Moments like that are an opportune time to find an alternative solution to a problem that the school did not know they had. It is also why combination tabletops are so useful.

Internal tabletops should be conducted at least once a year as well as combination tabletops. The frequency of testing is up to your school. Plan the tabletops well in advance for the scheduled date to mitigate any problems arising last minute, especially with combination tabletops. You are now inviting external stakeholders to the table. The last thing you want to do is look unorganized, waste their time, and ruin the relationship with them.

FULL SCALE EXERCISES

Typically, when people think about emergency exercises, they are thinking of full-scale exercises. Full-scale exercises are great because they now get the parts and personnel moving how your plan suggests along with the plans of all other stakeholders involved in the incident. While full-scale exercises seem to be the most practical, they also take the most time and money for which to plan.

The trend for schools right now in the 2010s is to practice active shooter scenarios. In the early 2000s, tornado and storm drills seemed to be the most popular. Whatever scenarios where schools feel they are most vulnerable are probably going to be the full-scale exercise they conduct.

First responders usually love full-scale exercises because it allows them to practice their skills but on a much larger scale on an expanding incident. Usually, this group of people will be the most likely to be willing to be involved for the entirety of the planning process.

Some full-scale exercises get very involved with victims being painted to show injuries or sometimes even theater students construct their own injuries similar to a film setting. These large exercises can and should be a fun way to test your plan along with everyone else's plan.

The downside of full-scale exercises is that they usually take anywhere from twelve to eighteen months for which to plan. Much coordination is needed as far as assigning personnel specifically designated to the mock incident, having the resources on scene that would normally be there during that incident, and so forth. Be patient with first responders when planning a full-scale exercise. If they are a paid department, they must find personnel to fill the shifts that are normal for that day, they also must make sure they have enough vehicles. If they are volunteer, they are more than likely going to have to take off work, find a babysitter, or both. Planning for these events can be very complex, but it most certainly is possible.

Money is also a factor for these large exercises. Some organizations may choose to send you a bill to pay for their personnel being there that day, others may send you a bill for equipment you asked to use. Ask these questions up front so that there is no awkward explanation needed to be had with the school board about large bills from the full-scale exercise that the school did not know about up front. Depending on your teachers' union they may asked to be compensated if they are not within "work hours." That is another hurdle to jump through before getting too far along in the planning process.

USE STAFF IN-SERVICE DAYS

Every school or district has days where staff is required to show up for work without students being at school. Some of these days are full days, some of these days are half days. An important element in creating your emergency preparedness culture is utilizing these days for small time periods to get your staff thinking about emergency preparedness on some level.

Have your emergency preparedness committee develop material for several one-hour-long workshops throughout your in-service days with different groups. Use your time wisely. It is not realistic to believe that a staff could or would want to gather for an entire in-service day to go over emergency preparedness. However, if you can deliver short bursts of information at a time, the staff will likely take in more information over a period of time.

CHAPTER 10 SUMMARY

Exercises are an ideal method for testing your finished emergency plans. In order to truly test your plans, your staff must know and understand what the plans are. If the plan is not shared, there is no reason to test your plan. Share the plan with your staff, test it, make necessary changes, and then test it again.

Before jumping right to a full-scale exercise, consider using workshops and tabletops to test your plan. It would be very frustrating to plan a full-scale exercise over eighteen months and then afterward realize that you wasted all that time because nobody knew your plan. Use logic in your planning and then test that logic before moving on.

The emergency preparedness cycle is never ending. You can never be too prepared. The exact plans will not matter during an emergency. When an emergency occurs, your staff will revert back to the training that they have had. If they have not been trained or tested, do not expect anything other than uncontrolled chaos. Emergencies are not in your favor, but how your people respond could be.

CHAPTER 10 PERSONAL INVENTORY

1) What types of exercises does your school currently conduct?
2) What types of exercises do you think your school would benefit from?
3) Has your school ever conducted a full-scale exercise?
    a. Was it effective?

Chapter Eleven

The Prepared School You Hope to Become

Not all change is progress, but all progress is the result of change.

—Coach John Wooden

It does not matter where your school is in its emergency planning process. The important piece is that you and your school get started. This process is not an overnight sensation. It will take time to get to where you want to be.

Surely, you and your emergency planning committee have an end result in mind. More than likely it is a cultural change you are seeking first before creating too many plans. Throughout the course of your initial emergency planning, it is important to create goals and set objectives to reach those goals.

If you are facing an organization that is resisting change, stay away from trying to shove a culture down their throats. If you are facing a resisting school district, you are going to be told no many times. Find ways around those no's so that next time it has the potential to become a yes. Try to win frequent small battles rather than few big battles. Small battles help people understand the importance of emergency planning. Big battles can be too much for some organizations.

If you are with a school that has its arms wide open waiting for change, your approach should not be much different; however, the reasoning for that pace is different. A school that wants change is a good thing. What has the potential of happening is that school takes in too much change that it is overwhelming and people become stressed. You too should celebrate small battles that are won. This is not a sprint, there is no end. It is a nice light jog.

It is impossible to plan for every single scenario. Create plans so that they can be adapted for many incidents. Practice these plans and welcome any ideas that could improve your plans. Your job is not to create a prison for your staff and students, but they must also understand that your school is not a free-for-all. You must find the happy medium in protecting your students and staff but also create an atmosphere that promotes learning, understanding, inspiration, and tolerance.

START YOUR COMMITTEE

The biggest part of starting is to have a committee. Do not just have this committee to have a committee. This committee is essentially a support group. When someone has a bad day trying to convince the community or leadership of something that needs to be done, that concern can be brought to the group. Many minds are better than one and many hands make a lighter load.

Use the people in your committee to lean on. More than likely this culture change is going to stress you out and will make you want to quit altogether. Remember why you started. If it takes a different approach or a change in plans, then do whatever is necessary to get the right people on board with your emergency planning and training efforts.

CONDUCT A RISK ASSESSMENT

This risk assessment is not to be conducted for added monotonous work or for additional paperwork. This risk assessment is needed to identify where your risks lie and what your greatest probabilities and vulnerabilities are. Treat it as such. Whether you choose to conduct a risk assessment in your own way or hire a contractor to do it for you, just get it done so you know what emergencies are statistically most likely to occur at your school.

This risk assessment can also be presented to anyone who is asking what is being planned for and why. It is a great tool to update your school board with and should be briefly presented to keep their attention.

WHAT YOUR SCHOOL NEEDS

By taking the next steps toward preparedness, your school needs honesty from those who are taking on the responsibility of emergency preparedness. Honesty is needed in conversations, reviews, assessments, conclusions, and fears. This is an uncomfortable conversation for many, but those who share their thoughts will breathe easier knowing that they shared their fears and possible solutions.

Honesty is also needed in your risk assessments. Assessments must be made on incidents that can *actually* affect your school's daily operations. Do not avoid the incidents that could cause the most damage, and likewise, do not avoid assessing the incidents that interrupt the school day the most. Be honest.

WHAT YOUR SCHOOL DOES *NOT* NEED

During any phase of your preparedness efforts, be careful not to get caught up with what is being done by schools around you. What works for one school may not work for another. It is okay to research ideas that are being used by other schools, but just because a neighboring school is buying metal detectors for all of their campuses, does not mean that is what your school needs.

Again, this is where the risk assessment is crucial. If your school already has a lot of peer-to-peer violence during the school day, you may need to look into more physical security, monitoring systems, metal detectors, and school resource officers. However, if your school is typically a school that does not have many incidents, large investments into airport-type security measures may not be necessary. Maybe your school just needs a paradigm shift in its preparedness culture or some updated policies.

No matter what decision your school makes as far as investing in equipment or people, just know that it is just another tool in the tool box. You would not use an axe to hammer a nail, just as you should not expect metal detectors to respond to bomb threats.

Another commonality in schools is whatever the hot topic is (active shooter, bomb threats, etc.) that is the only incident they will prepare for. Your plans should be comprehensive and should cover more than just one or two scenarios.

MAKE THE PLAN

When writing the actual plans for scenarios determined by your risk assessments, be brief but say what needs to be said. You want your policies to spell out what is expected and planned for, but getting into the weeds and being too detailed could cause confusion and miscommunications.

Be sure to include the introduction pieces and the promulgation. Having those documents and showing that your school board and district leaders support you by having signed their approval is a good reminder for them of why they need to be involved and it also is a huge part of gaining top-down support.

With each step you take toward becoming a fun, yet safer, school, the closer you are to becoming the school you saw when you first began the emergency planning process. Protect your staff and support them. Find the happy medium between Disneyland and a prison. Your staff are the people who inspire everyday learning so that we can create a world that is safe, healthy, friendly, and knowledgeable. Protect your students because they are your responsibility. It goes without saying that your students are someone else's child, they mean the whole world to someone else. They are the future.

You can become the safe school you have envisioned. It is going to take time, it is going to take healthy and honest discussions, and it is going to take a culture change. You will need the support of your leaders. Once you have that, the opportunity is yours for the taking. Don't miss it. Go out there and make our schools a better place. One small battle at a time.

References

Adesman, Andrew, & Schapiro, L. Exponential, not addictive, increase in risk of weapons carrying by adolescents who themselves are frequent and recurrent victims of bullying.

Blair, J. Pete, & Schweit, Katherine W. (2014). A study of active shooter incidents, 2000–2013. Texas State University and the Federal Bureau of Investigation, U.S. Department of Justice, Washington, D.C., 2014.

Council of State Governments Justice Center. (2014, February). *School safety plans: A snapshot of legislative action*. New York: Council of State Governments Justice Center.

FEMA. (n.d.). ICS Organization. Retrieved from https://training.fema.gov/emiweb/is/icsresource/assets/icsorganization.pdf

Florida Statute, K-20 Education Code, Support for Learning, Chapter 1006, Section 07.

Florida Department of Education. (2012). *District safety & security best practices*. Retrieved from http://www.fldoe.org/finance/emergency-management/dis-safety-security-best-practices.stml

Ove, T. (2015, February). Suspect in 2012 Pitt bomb threats extradited from Ireland to Scotland. *Pittsburgh Post-Gazette*. Retrieved from http://www.post-gazette.com/local/city/2015/02/20/Suspect-in-2012-Pitt-bomb-threats-extradited-from-Ireland-to-Scotland/stories/201502200289

Owens Community College. (2017). Bomb threat & suspicious package/letter. Retrieved from https://www.owens.edu/emergency/bomb.html

Philpott, D., & Serluco, P. (2009). *Public school emergency preparedness and crisis management plan*. Lanham, MD: Government Institutes.

Santiago, C. (2017, April). Emergency preparedness for students with special needs. *ASBO International's School Business Affairs, 83*(4), 36–37.

A timeline of Pitt's bomb threats. (2012, April 22). *Pitt News*.

U.S. Department of Education, Office of Elementary and Secondary Education, & Office of Safe and Healthy Students. (2013). *Guide for developing high-quality school emergency operations plan*. Washington, D.C.: U.S. Department of Education.

U.S. Department of Homeland Security, Federal Emergency Management Institute. (2008). EOC management and operations independent study course.

U.S. Department of Homeland Security, Federal Emergency Management Institute. (2013). IS 362.A—Multi-hazard emergency planning for schools. Retrieved from https://training.fema.gov/is/courseoverview.aspx?code=is-362.a

Index

active shooters, 7; bomb threats with, 45; bullied students as, 49; EOC for, 68; FBI on percentage school, 41; full-scale exercises on, 74; templated plans responding to, 41–42; wounded on folding tables after, 36
administrative assistants, 36
administrative days, 4, 74–75
administrators, 10–11, 14, 18; concerns brought to, 3; culture change from top, 17; special event risks and planning by, 53
annexes, 31
annex maps, 31
Arizona, 31

background security, 54–56
basic plan, 30–31
BERT. *See* Building Emergency Response Team
Bomb Threat Checklist, 43, *44*, 45
bomb threats, *9*, 42–45; metal detectors not responding to, 78
buddy system, 50
Building Emergency Response Team (BERT), 36–39; identification and request room in, 47
bullying programs, 49
burning house down scenarios, 5, 25–26

bus drivers, 3, 59–61, 63
bus emergencies, 57–59, 62
buses: evacuation use of, 38–39; insurance risk and, 58; state laws exceeded for, 51, 60; timelines protecting arrivals of, 55
business administrators, 14
buy in: CMT needing, 66–67; EOP with top down, 30–31; exercises for, 72; plans needing, 78

cafeteria supervisors, 4
case studies, 10
chain of command: BERT with, 37–38; EOP for, 6; ICS and roles in, 20–21, *21*
checkpoints, 53
chief executive officers, 14
CMT. *See* crisis management team
Collective Bargaining Agreements, 4
command staff, 23, *23*
committees, 4–7; Arizona requiring planning, 31; CMT as safety, 66; exercises planned by, 71; as support group, 77
communications: ICS improving, 27; liaison officers in, *23*, 24; operational security plan in, 54
consultants, 12; exercises planned by, 71; risk assessment with, 8, *9*

Council of State Governments (CSG), 31
credentialing, 55–56
crisis management team (CMT):
  accident history reviewed by, 8–9,
  9, 66; buy in and remediation for,
  66–67; faculty starting, 69
CSG. *See* Council of State Governments
culture change, 16; emergency
  preparedness in, 33, 70; overwhelm
  avoided on, 76; safe school from, 79;
  top administrators for starting, 17–18
custodians, 4, 36

drills and practice, 27; bus emergencies
  in, 58–59; fire drills in, 40; full-scale
  exercises as, 73; plans and, 42, 76

EMA. *See* Emergency Management
  Agency
emergencies: BERT type of, 37; bullying
  and creation of, 49; go-bags for special
  needs students in, 50; IC for school,
  22, *22*; important items in, 39; most
  and least prepared for, 51; necessary
  actions in, 35; parent-student
  reunification in, 45–49; plans tested
  for, 64; response teams for, 36–37;
  roles known in, 63; special events and,
  52; special needs students in, 49; staff
  reversion to training in, 75; training on
  plans for, 70; types of, 7–10, 40
Emergency Management Agency
  (EMA), 29
emergency operations centers (EOC),
  67–69
emergency operations plan (EOP):
  chain of command for, 6; ICS and
  plain language in, 34; school politics
  influencing, 14; state requirements
  on school districts and, 31; statistics
  predicting for, 33; as tailored for
  school, 29–30
emergency plans, 3–5; buy-in for, 78;
  complacency and laziness influencing,
  16–17; exercises for improvement of,

71; Florida outline for school, 31–33,
  32; goals and objectives for, 76; ICS
  for, 20; MACC for testing, 68–69; not
  publicly posting, 7; on-site and off-
  site reunification, 48; prisons avoided
  with, 41, 76–77; school district
  officials involved in, 17–18; school
  funding and, 14–15; testing of, 64,
  72, 75; training on, 70; types of, 7–10,
  40; workshops and tabletops
  for sharing, 75
emergency questions, 25
emergency response resources, 19
EOC. *See* emergency operations centers
EOP. *See* emergency operations plan
evacuation, 40; bigger attack set up
  from, 45; buses used in, 38–39
evaluator, 72
exercises, 71–75. *See also* drills and
  practice; testing
exposures, 10

faculty, 28; CMT started by, 69; IC as
  any, 22
Federal Bureau of Investigation (FBI), 41
Federal Emergency Management
  Agency (FEMA), 26–28, 68; EOP and
  guidelines by, 34; ICS developed by, 20
fencing, 53
finance/administrative, *24*, 25
fire drills, 40
firefighters, 7, 17, 19
fires, *9*
first aid, 38
first responders: committee involvement
  for, 6; faculty preparing with, 28;
  firefighters as, 7, *9*, 17, 19; ICS
  differences of schools and, 26;
  resource management with, 19–20
floor plans, 31
Florida, 31–33, *32*
full-scale exercises, 73–74

goals, 5–6
go-bags, 50

grief rooms, *46*, 46–48
guidance counselors, 3, 36

Health Insurance Portability and Accountability Act, 7
history, 8–9, *9*, 66
hospital staff, 7

IC. *See* incident commander
ICS. *See* Incident Command System
incident commander (IC): cross-training for, 27; delegation by, 23; ICS leader as, 20; school boards not needing, 26; for school emergency, 22, *22*
Incident Command System (ICS): chain defining roles in, 20–22, *21*; drills on school objectives in, 27; EOP with plain language and, 34; faculty filling positions of, 28; placing staff in, 35; responsibilities in, *24*, 24–25; school operations in, 26
in-service days. *See* administrative days
insurance companies, 7; risk and, 58, 60
interruption strength, 8–9, *9*

Justice Center, of CSG, 31

liaison officers, *23*, 23–24
lockdowns, 40, 42; annexes with instructions for, 31; medications missed during, 50
lock-outs, 40

MACC. *See* Multi-Agency Coordination Centers
media, 23, *23*, 67
medical emergency, *9*
medications, 50
metal detectors, 78
Multi-Agency Coordination Centers (MACC), 67–69

National Incident Management System (NIMS), 20
nurses, 4, 36

operational security, 54
operations chief, *24*, 24–25

parent/guardian entrance, *46*, 46–47
parent reunification, 7; BERT activated for, 37; students in, 45–49
parents, 3, 16; bus emergencies and, 58; social media posts and inquiries by, 59; special needs students planning with, 50
parent-teacher organizations (PTO/PTA), 16
peer pressure, 49
peer-to-peer violence, 78
personal agendas, 15–16
physical security, 53
planning needs, 10; more than one scenario for, 40, 78; shooter and lone wolf as difficult in, 42
police, 7; emergency response resources for, 19; events including, 48, 53; liaison officer communicating with, 23, 24
policies, 78; transportation and safety, 61, 63
politics, 14, 18
preparedness, 3, 13, 51; administrators and, 10–11; measuring culture of, 33, 70; staff in-service days for, 74
presentations, 10–12, 77
principals, 14, 36
probability of risk, 8–9, *9*
PTO/PTA. *See* parent-teacher organizations
public information officers, 23, *23*, 67. *See also* liaison officers

Red Cross, *23*, 24
reputation loss, 65–66
request room, *46*, 46–47
rescue, 38
response teams, 36–37
reunification. *See* parent reunification
reunification area, 46, *46*
risk, 8–9, *9*; buses and insurance, 58; culture change and creation of, 16–17

risk assessments, 76; biggest risks found in, 8–9, *9*; honesty needed in, 77; insurance companies for, 60; planning determined by, 40; reunification activation from, 46; school boards presented with, 10–11, 77; school buses and, 58; school peer pressure avoided with, 78

risk events, 8–9, *9*, 66

runners, 47

safety concerns, 11, 78

safety officer, *23*, 24

scenarios, 3; bomb threats and response, 43, 45; buses and crash, 58–59; EOP for, 6; planning for multiple, 40, 78; school district officials with, 14; teachers presented with vulnerable, 5; testing exercises for, 72; training and multiple, 51

school. *See specific topics*

school boards: IC not needed by, 26; risk assessment presented to, 10–11, 77; vested groups heard by, 16

school district officials, 3; buses controlled by, 58; culture changing and backing by, 16–19; EOP and state requirements by, 31; exposure and vulnerability views by, 14; reputation loss response by, 65–66; templated plans tailored for, 42

school funding, 14–15, 18

secure exit, 46, *46*

shelter, 7

shelter-in-place, 31, 40, 42

shootings. *See active shooters*

signage, 53

social media: posts on, 3, 59, 63; public information officer monitoring, 23, *23*; updating information via, 48

soft targets, 17

special events, 52–53, 56

special interest groups. *See* vested interest groups

special needs students, 49–50

staff, 36, 78; committees and hospital, 7; ICS and, *23–24*, 23–25; parent reunification testing of, 48; politics and process overlooked by, 18; preparation and days for, 74; training for support of, 75

state laws, 34; Arizona and Florida with, 31–33, *32*; meeting and exceeding, 51, 60

students, 78–79; BERT and, 36–37; tracking of, 48, 62–63; weapons brought by bullied, 49

student staging room, *46*, 46–47

superintendents, 14

tabletop exercises, 72–73, 75

teachers, 3–5, 19; BERT position as, 36; ICS and, 20–21; vested interest group as, 16

teamwork, 38

templated plans, 41–42

terrorists, 42

testing: emergency plans and, 64, 72, 75; EOCs and MACCs in, 68–69; parent reunification process, 45, 48

timelines, 54–55, 67

training, 70, 75; BERT as special operations in, 38; ICs and cross-, 27; multiple scenarios in, 51

transportation, 7, 61; exceed state laws for bus, 51, 60; school responsibility in, 57

transportation risk management, 60–63

unified command (UC), 26

unions, 4, 16, 74

vested interest groups, 16, 18

weapons, 49

workshops, 71–72, 74–75

About the Author

Cody M. Santiago is an emergency preparedness professional that specializes in educational institutions. Mr. Santiago has traveled across the United States to work with many schools of all sizes to improve their emergency preparedness. He has worked with schools to evaluate potential risks and vulnerabilities, turning their fears into motivation to create plans for prevention, mitigation, response, and recovery.

Mr. Santiago has earned his B.S. in homeland security from California University of Pennsylvania and is currently pursuing his M.S. in enterprise risk management from Boston University. In a world where risk management is critical in schools, Mr. Santiago seeks to provide helpful insight to educators and administrators in how schools can create a culture of preparedness.

Creating a culture that is receptive to responding to incidents, no matter how big or small they may be, could save lives. Schools across the country should embrace these concepts and exercise them regularly. This book will aid in your preparation and training of your coworkers and staff members while responding to an emergency, no matter the magnitude. Mr. Santiago's knowledge and logic are useful tools to use, not only in our schools but also in our daily lives.

www.ingramcontent.com/pod-product-compliance
Lightning Source LLC
Chambersburg PA
CBHW030118010526
44116CB00005B/308